ULTIMATE BRAINBUSTER | GENERAL KNOWLEDGE QUIZ BOOK

HOWARD BYROM

ILLUSTRATIONS by VICTORIA WAINWRIGHT

Published by Igloo Books Limited
Henson Way
Telford Way Industrial Estate
Kettering
Northants
NN16 8PX

info@igloo-books.com

This edition published 2005

ISBN 1-84561-199-3

Project management: Kandour Ltd
Editorial and design management: boxedBRAND
Author: Howard Byrom
Illustrations: Victoria Wainwright
Cover design: Peter Gates
Production: Sophy Colbert

ULTIMATE
BRAINBUSTER
CONTENTS

ULTIMATE BRAINBUSTER GENERAL KNOWLEDGE QUIZ BOOK

ROUND 1

FOOD & DR

NK

ROUND 1
FOOD & DRINK 1

QUESTIONS

1. Which restaurant was Jamie Oliver working in before becoming a TV star?
2. Which restaurant critic took over from Jonathan Meades in The Times?
3. What temperature does water boil at?
4. The process where foods brown during cooking is known as what?
5. In which alcoholic drink might you find a worm?
6. Saffron comes from the stamen of which flower?
7. Rioja comes from which country?
8. Capers are derived from what?
9. Which supermarket is Jamie Oliver the face of?
10. A skillet is a pan generally made from which material?

ANSWERS

1. River Cafe
2. Giles Coren
3. 100 degrees C
4. Maillard Reaction
5. Mescal
6. Crocus
7. Spain
8. The pickled flower buds of a Mediterranean plant
9. Sainsbury's
10. Cast Iron

ROUND 1
FOOD & DRINK 2

QUESTIONS

1. Which order of friars is coffee topped with steamed milk named after?
2. A tagine is a speciality dish of which country?
3. A dining chair with arms is known as a what?
4. Sea urchin sushi is known as what in Japanese?
5. Forks were originally known as what?
6. The prongs on a fork are known as what?
7. Approximately how many coffee beans make up an espresso measure?
8. A cappuccino coffee is named after what?
9. What is the annual yield of a single coffee plant?
10. What percentage of total production does the Arabic coffee bean represent?

ANSWERS

1. Capuchin
2. Morocco
3. Carver
4. Uni
5. Splitspoons
6. Tines
7. 40
8. Monks
9. 1kg
10. 70%

ROUND 1
FOOD & DRINK 3

QUESTIONS

1. Armagnac is a brandy originating from which part of France?
2. What wine is traditionally matched with pate and brioche?
3. What is the main ingredient in advocaat?
4. What is the earliest known cereal to be cultivated?
5. What is the name of a dish of cold meat served in aspic?
6. The dish of rice, flaked fish, and hard-boiled eggs is known as what?
7. The aperitif made from white Aligote wine and cassis is known as what?
8. Food that is permitted to be eaten according to Jewish dietary laws is known as what?
9. Which American chef wrote Kitchen Confidential?
10. The stomach of a cow or sheep is known as what?

ANSWERS

1. Gascony
2. Sauternes
3. Egg yolk
4. Barley
5. Ballottine
6. Kedgeree
7. Kir
8. Kosher
9. Anthony Bourdain
10. Tripe

ROUND 1
FOOD & DRINK 4

QUESTIONS

1. The subterranean fungus highly prized in cooking is known as what?
2. Caviar comes from which fish?
3. What bird is traditionally eaten for Thanksgiving?
4. The vanilla plant is native to which country?
5. Valpoliccella is red wine from which region of Italy?
6. The finest strands of pasta are known as what?
7. Toasted bread covered with a mixture of cheese, pale ale, and mustard is known as what?
8. The marine snail is better known as what?
9. The Italian desert made by whisking egg yolks, wine, and sugar is known as what?
10. What is the name of the baked batter portions traditionally served with roast beef in Britain?

ANSWERS

1. Truffle
2. Sturgeon
3. Turkey
4. Mexico
5. Veneto
6. Vermicelli
7. Welsh Rarebit
8. Whelk
9. Zabaglione
10. Yorkshire pudding

ROUND 1
FOOD & DRINK 5

QUESTIONS

1. Foie gras is the liver of which animal?
2. Who was the first man to bring cocoa beans to Europe?
3. White Russian cocktails are made from milk, vodka, and which liqueur?
4. Goose is known as what in France?
5. Which nation eats the most chocolate per capita?
6. What is the alcoholic ingredient in a Bloody Mary?
7. The main ingredient in a black pudding is what?
8. Which ancient Central American civilisation were drinking chocolate milk as long ago as 600BC?
9. Which chef created Peach Melba, in honour of the Australian opera singer?
10. Cumberland sauce is a is traditionally served cold with what?

ANSWERS

1. Goose
2. Juan de Cardenas
3. Kahlua
4. Foie
5. Switzerland
6. Vodka
7. Pig blood
8. Mayans
9. Escoffier
10. Venison

ROUND 1
FOOD & DRINK 6

QUESTIONS

1. The process where starch swells when cooked in water is called what?
2. What temperature do green vegetables begin to discolour?
3. What temperature do egg whites begin to coagulate?
4. What temperature do yolks begin to set?
5. Pasta is a starchy food made from egg and what?
6. What is the chemical contained in onions that brings tears to your eyes?
7. In 2001 what dish was declared Britain's most popular?
8. What year were tin-free steel cans introduced?
9. What year did the first ever McDonalds open?
10. What years did wartime food rationing end in Britain

ANSWERS

1. Gelatinisation
2. 66°C
3. 60°C
4. 65°C
5. Wheat
6. Sulphur
7. Chicken Tikka Masala
8. 1965
9. 1954
10. 1951

ROUND 1
FOOD & DRINK 7

QUESTIONS

1. Daquiris are cocktails based around which spirit?
2. Garlic is known as what in Spain?
3. The words Grande Toque mean what?
4. How heavy is the world's largest chocolate bar, listed in the Guinness Book of Records?
5. What is a thin slice of pork or chicken breast known as?
6. Drambuie is a liqueur originating from which country?
7. Schnitzel is traditionally made from what kind of meat?
8. Traditional Scots porridge is made from which cereal?
9. Feijoada. A stew made from pork and beans, is associated with which nation
10. Bearnaise sauce is made with vinegar, butter, and what?

ANSWERS

1. Rum
2. Ajo
3. Head Chef
4. 2280kg
5. Escalope
6. Scotland
7. Veal
8. Oats
9. Brazil
10. Egg yolks

ROUND 1
FOOD & DRINK 8

QUESTIONS

1. Tournedos Rossini is a dish made from fillet steak, black truffles, and what other ingredient?
2. Who perfected the extraction of cocoa butter from cocoa beans in 1825?
3. Chateaubriand is a dish made from what?
4. At what temperature does cocoa butter melt?
5. What sauce is Chateaubriand traditionally served with?
6. What is correct name for the shallow silver receptacles commonly used by wine tasters?
7. Sacher Torte is a chocolate tart named after a hotel in which European city?
8. Parsley is known as what in France?
9. What year was Cadbury the British confectioners founded?
10. Garlic is known as what in France?

ANSWERS

1. Foie gras
2. Conrad Van Houten
3. Fillet steak
4. 37°c
5. Béarnaise
6. Tate-vin
7. Vienna
8. Persil
9. 1824
10. Ail

ROUND 1
FOOD & DRINK 9

QUESTIONS

1. Tzatziki is a Greek dish made from yoghurt, mint, cucumber and which other ingredient?
2. Confit is a method of cooking where the main ingredient is cooked and preserved in what?
3. A wine waiter is known as what?
4. Sherry is named after which Spanish town?
5. Pate de Canard is made from which animal?
6. Tournedos Rossini is a dish made from filet steak, fois gras, and which other ingredient?
7. Apart from rice the main ingredient in a risotto is what?
8. What are the ingredients of a Kir Royale?
9. What are the ingredients of a Martini?
10. What is the main ingredients of a black pudding?

ANSWERS

1. Garlic
2. Fat
3. Sommelier
4. Jerez (de Frontera)
5. Duck
6. Truffles
7. Stock
8. Champagne and Cassis
9. Gin, vermouth, olive
10. Pig's blood

ROUND 1
FOOD & DRINK 10

QUESTIONS

1. Chlodnik is an iced soup from which European country?
2. The food critics, Gault and Millau were responsible for which food movement?
3. The average Swiss citizen eats how much chocolate every year?
4. Nuits-Saint-George is a wine producing village in which French region?
5. A Negroni is made from equal measures of gin, vermouth, and what other alcoholic beverage?
6. Leek and potato soup thickened with cream and served cold is known as what?
7. A Manhattan is based around vermouth and what spirit?
8. Which Swiss confectioner is responsible for developing milk chocolate?
9. The legendary French Chef, August Escoffier, presided over the kitchens of which London hotel?

ANSWERS

1. Poland
2. Nouvelle Cuisine
3. 10kg
4. Burgundy
5. Campari
6. Vichyssoise
7. Rye whisky
8. Daniel Peter
9. Savoy
10. Burgundy

ROUND 1

FOOD & DRINK 11

QUESTIONS

1. Balsamic vinegar is closely associated with which Italian city?
2. A dish of raw fish marinated in lemon juice is known as what?
3. Courgettes are known as what in Italy?
4. Tapas are bar snacks originating from which country?
5. The freshwater crustacean that resembles lobster is called what?
6. The traditional Spanish dish of rice, stock, meat and fish is known as what?
7. Paella originates from what region of Spain?
8. The traditional Italian dish of rice, stock, butter, and Parmesan cheese is known as what?
9. Parmesan cheese orginates from which Italian city?
10. Raw and cured meat is known as what in Italy?

ANSWERS

1. Modena
2. Ceviche
3. Zucchini
4. Spain
5. Crayfish
6. Paella
7. Albufera
8. Risotto
9. Parma
10. Salami

ROUND 1
FOOD & DRINK 12

QUESTIONS

1. What is the world's biggest selling chocolate bar?
2. Which river is port most famously associated with?
3. Chateau d'Yquem is most famous for what?
4. Nigella is better known as which herb?
5. Which Portuguese city does port take its name from?
6. Pont-l'Eveque cheese is from which region in France?
7. Which pioneering Swiss confectioner began adding extra cocoa butter to make it smoother and glossier?
8. Pont-l'Eveque cheese is made from the milk of which animal?
9. What's the name for the procedure of cooking food by gently simmering it in a liquid?
10. When was milk chocolate first developed?

ANSWERS

1. Kit Kat
2. Douro
3. Sweet white wine
4. Fennel
5. Oporto
6. Normandy
7. Rudolphe Lindt
8. Cow
9. Poaching
10. 1875

ROUND 1
FOOD & DRINK 13

QUESTIONS

1. Lamb's fry refers to which part of a sheep? .
2. What cooking implement has China given the culinary world?
3. Salvatore Calabrese is the famous cocktail master at which famous London hotel?
4. Which restaurant is believed to be London's oldest?
5. What was Jeffrey Dahmer's last meal?
6. What animal is traditionally used to find truffles?
7. The white of an egg is called what?
8. The spoon traditionally used to stir porridge is called what?
9. Gin is a spirit flavoured which berry?
10. High class London restaurant, Le Gavroche, is home to which family of chefs?

ANSWERS

1. Testicles
2. Wok
3. The Lanesborough
4. Rules
5. A hard boiled egg, toast, cereal and coffee
6. Pig
7. Albumen
8. Spirtle
9. Juniper
10. Roux Brothers

ROUND 1
FOOD & DRINK 14

QUESTIONS

1. A Tom Collins is made from lemon juice, soda, and which spirit?
2. Cassoulet is a traditional stew originating from what part of France?
3. Cassis is a liqueur is made from what?
4. Chop Suey – a dish of chopped simmered vegetables - originated in which country?
5. Which famous chef wrote Le Guide Culinaire in 1903?
6. Apart from champagne, what other alcoholic ingredient is used in a champagne cocktail?
7. Chorizo is a sausage originating from which country?
8. AOC Paulliac, the appellation famous for claret, is located in which south-western French wine region?
9. Cider is produced from what?
10. The process of cooking duck or goose legs in fat before storing them is called what?

ANSWERS

1. Gin
2. Languedoc
3. Blackcurrants
4. USA
5. Escoffier
6. Cognac
7. Spain
8. Haut-Medoc
9. Apples
10. Confit

ROUND 1

FOOD & DRINK 15

QUESTIONS

1. The Italian dish ossobuco is made from what meat?
2. In Scotland, stuffed braised chicken is known as what?
3. The brewery at St James's Gate in Dublin is home to which beer?
4. What is the Scandinavian method of curing salmon called?
5. The Swedish tradition of presenting a buffet of numerous small dishes is called what?
6. Emmental cheese comes from which country?
7. Russian beetroot soup is known as what?
8. Paprika is closely associated with which eastern European country?
9. Traditional air-dried Swiss meat is known as what?
10. What German dish is made from salted strips of white cabbage?

ANSWERS

1. Veal
2. Howtowdie
3. Guinness
4. Gravlaks
5. Smorgasbord
6. Switzerland
7. Borscht
8. Hungary
9. Bunder Fleisch
10. Sauerkraut

ROUND 1
FOOD & DRINK 16

QUESTIONS

1. Chassagne-Montrachet is a famous wine-producing village in which French region?
2. An estate or plantation given over to the production of wine in France is known as what?
3. The person in charge of the dining area of a restaurant is known as what?
4. What year did Cadbury's 'Dairy Milk' appear?
5. A magret is the breast of which animal?
6. Mace is a spice derived from what?
7. What year did Rudolphe Lindt perfects a recipe for fondant chocolate?
8. Nutmeg originates from where?
9. When did the Nouvelle Cuisine movement begin?
10. Chateau d'Yquem is in which French region?

ANSWERS

1. Burgundy
2. Chateau
3. Maitre d'hôtel
4. 1905
5. Duck
6. Nutmeg seed
7. 1879
8. Indonesia
9. 1972
10. Bordeaux

ROUND 1
FOOD & DRINK 17

QUESTIONS

1. How many milligrams of caffeine does one ounce of chocolate contain?
2. The Australian opera singer, Dame Nellie Melba, leant her name to what famous dessert?
3. What is the world record for drinking a 400ml bottle of ketchup through a straw?
4. What percentage is the sugar content of a ripe banana?
5. The tomato originates in which South American country?
6. A chef's hat is known as what?
7. What year was the first cookery book produced?
8. Who wrote the world's first cookery book?
9. How much do consumers in the UK spend on food annually?
10. What temperature does the Maillard reaction process begin to brown cooking food?

ANSWERS

1. 20
2. Peach Melba
3. 33 seconds
4. 20%
5. Peru
6. A toque
7. 1651
8. François de la Varenne
9. £53 billion
10. 154°C

ROUND 1
FOOD & DRINK 18

QUESTIONS

1. Clear meat, poultry, or fish stock traditionally served at the beginning of a meal is known as what?
2. Boudin Noir is known as what in English?
3. Bouillabaisse is closely associated with which French city?
4. A traditional Martini cocktail is made from vermouth, an olive, and which spirit?
5. Stuffed vine leaves are known as what?
6. Sugared almonds are known as what in France?
7. Buck's Fizz is better known as what in America?
8. What is the UK's most popular chocolate bar?
9. What's the name of an establishment where livestock is slaughtered?
10. What do the letters AOC on a bottle of French wine stand for?

ANSWERS

1. Consommé
2. Black Pudding
3. Marseilles
4. Gin
5. Dolmades
6. Dragee
7. Mimosa
8. Cadbury's 'Dairy Milk'
9. Abattoir
10. Appellation d'Origin Controlee

ULTIMATE BRAINBUSTER

ROUND 2
FILM & TV

ROUND 2
FILM & TV 1

QUESTIONS

1. What is the London square featured in Eastenders?
2. Who played Eleanor Ewing in the TV series Dallas?
3. What was the name of the group of scantily clad ladies in 'The Benny Hill Show'?
4. Who played Mr Drysdale's secretary, Janet Trego in 'The Beverly Hillbillies'?
5. John Thaw and Dennis Waterman are best remembered es as Jack Regan and George Carter in which TV cop show?
6. What is the pub called in 'Coronation Street'?
7. Which 1982 British movie featured 300,000 extras?
8. What year was the first episode of 'Armchair Thriller' shown? .
9. In the TV series 'Dad's Army' which private had been excused from the real army due to his unusual blood type?
10. Which character did John Forsythe play in the TV series 'Dallas'?

ANSWERS

1. Albert Square
2. Barbara Bel Geddes
3. Hills Angels
4. Sharon Tate
5. The Sweeney
6. The Rovers Return
7. Gandhi
8. 1978
9. Private Pike
10. Blake Carrington

ROUND 2
FILM & TV 2

QUESTIONS

1. Who played Alexis Carrington's nemesis Krystle in the hit TV show 'Dynasty'?
2. Who played Major Anthony Nelson in the 1960s TV show 'I dream of Jeannie'?
3. In the hit TV show Dallas who was a former Miss Texas?
4. Who directed 'Marnie' in 1964?
5. Who plays Margo Channing, an aging theatre star in the 1950 film 'All about Eve'?
6. Who was born Norma Jeane Mortensen on June 1 1926?
7. Who is the most remembered star of 'Rebel Without a Cause'?
8. Who was the young female star of the 1943 film 'Lassie Come Home'?
9. Who played Dorothy in 'The Wizard of Oz'?
10. Who was played the lead role of Samantha Stephens in US TV show 'Bewitched'?

ANSWERS

1. Linda Evans
2. Larry Hagman
3. Sue Ellen
4. Alfred Hitchcock
5. Bette Davis
6. Marilyn Monroe
7. James Dean
8. Elizabeth Taylor
9. Judy Garland
10. Elizabeth Montgomery

ROUND 2
FILM & TV 3

QUESTIONS

1. What was the name of the invisible dog who sometimes appeared in the TV series 'I Dream of Jeannie'?
2. James Bolam and Rodney Bewes are better known as whom?
3. Pans People were dancers on which TV show?
4. In 1940 which Alfred Hitchcock film won the Best Picture Oscar?
5. In 1978 which film, starring Robert De Niro won the Best Picture Oscar?
6. Who presented 'The Old Grey Whistle Test'?
7. Who plays the female lead in the 1997 movie 'Titanic'?
8. Who is the robot in 'Buck Rogers in the 25th Century'?
9. In May of 1962 who sang "Happy Birthday, Mr. President" at a televised birthday party for President John F. Kennedy?
10. In 1980 which film, directed by Robert Redford won the Best Picture Oscar?

ANSWERS

1. Djinn Djinn
2. The likely lads
3. Top of the Pops
4. Rebecca
5. The Deer Hunter
6. Bob Harris
7. Kate Winslet
8. Twiki
9. Marilyn Monroe
10. Ordinary People

ROUND 2
FILM & TV 4

QUESTIONS

1. What was unusual about the star of the 1960's hit TV show 'Mr Ed'?
2. Who took over as presenter of 'The Generation Game' in 1995?
3. In the hit TV show 'Dallas' who shot JR?
4. Eddie Waring, Stuart Hall and David Vine were commentators on which inter-town sport based TV show?
5. Which actor did Vivien Leigh marry on August 31st 1940?
6. In 1983 which film, starring Robert Redford won the Best Picture Oscar?
7. Who hosted 'Winner Takes All'
8. Which 1986 Vietnam war film was written and directed by Oliver Stone?
9. Which movie won 11 Academy Awards on March 23, 1998 including best picture of 1997?
10. How old was Jodie Foster when she played a prostitute in Martin Scorsese's film 'Taxi Driver'?

ANSWERS

1. He was a talking horse
2. Jim Davidson
3. Sue Ellen's sister Kristen Shepard
4. It's A Knockout
5. Laurence Olivier
6. Out of Africa
7. Jimmy Tarbuck
8. Platoon
9. Titanic
10. Fourteen

ROUND 2
FILM & TV 5

QUESTIONS

1. Who is the cannibal played by Anthony Hopkins in 'The Silence of the Lambs'?
2. What year did Eastenders begin?
3. Eamonn Andrews and his big red book was the host of which UK show?
4. Who directed the movie 'Jaws'?
5. In 1955 who's first starring role, was as Cal Trask in 'East of Eden'?
6. How long did the hit TV show 'Dynasty' run?
7. On which Hollywood actresses tombstone is written, "She did it the hard way"?
8. Who is the leading lady in the film 'The Birds'?
9. Who played Officer Stacey Sheridan in the US cop show 'T J Hooker'?
10. Who died in a road accident in a Porsche 550 Spyder near Salinas, California on September 30 1955, aged 24?

ANSWERS

1. Dr. Hannibal Lecter
2. 1985
3. This Is Your Life
4. Stephen Spielberg
5. James Dean
6. 8 years
7. Bette Davis
8. Tippi Hedren
9. Heather Locklear
10. James Dean

ROUND 2
FILM & TV 6

QUESTIONS

1. What was the name of the ranch where the Ewings lived in 'Dallas'?
2. What year was 'Coronation Street' first shown?
3. Which US children's TV show featured Gonzo, Waldorf, Swedish Chef and Animal?
4. Who directed the 1955 movie East of Eden?
5. In which film would you find the yellow brick road?
6. Who is the actress daughter of Alfred Hitchcock's leading lady Tippi Hedren?
7. Which 1956 film was James Dean nominated for an Academy Award for?
8. How many times has Elizabeth Taylor been married?
9. Which 1956 film tells the story of rival ranchers and oilmen in West Texas?
10. What year did Alfred Hitchcock receive an honorary Oscar?

ANSWERS

1. Southfork
2. 1960
3. The Muppets
4. Elia Kazan
5. The Wizard of Oz
6. Melanie Griffiths
7. Giant
8. 8 times
9. Giant
10. 1968

ROUND 2
FILM & TV 7

QUESTIONS

1. What year was the final episode of 'Dallas' shown?
2. The TV drama 'Angels' centred around which profession?
3. Who's catchphrase was "Nice to see you, to see you...nice"?
4. What was the name of the 'Angel' played by Kate Jackson in 'Charlie's Angels?
5. Which comedy legend is better know as Eric Bartholomew?
6. What year was The Walt Disney company founded?
7. In 1961 which film, starring Natalie Wood won ten Oscars including Best Picture Oscar?
8. Who played Scarlett O'Hara in the 1939 movie 'Gone with the Wind'?
9. What is Jaime Sommers better know as?
10. What was the original working title of the TV show 'Dynasty'?

ANSWERS

1. 1991
2. Nursing
3. Bruce Forsythe
4. Sabrina Duncan
5. Eric Morecambe
6. 1923
7. West Side Story
8. Vivien Leigh
9. The Bionic Woman
10. Oil

ROUND 2
FILM & TV 8

QUESTIONS

1. What was the name of Samantha's mother in hit TV show 'Bewitched'?
2. What was the name of Steptoe's horse in Steptoe and Son?
3. What year was 'Come Dancing' first shown?
4. What was the name of the 'Dallas' spin off TV show featuring Gary Ewing?
5. Which TV show featured John Cleese in the 'Mininstry of Silly Walks'?
6. In 1927 Walt Disney came up with the idea for an animated mouse who would become Mickey Mouse, but was he first called?
7. In 1971 which film, starring Gene Hackman won the Best Picture Oscar?
8. Which 80's hit TV show included royalty in its line up in the guise of Princess of Yugoslavia, Catherine Oxenberg?
9. Who won Best Actor Oscar in 2000?
10. Who was named Miss Artichoke in 1948?

ANSWERS

1. Endora
2. Hercules
3. 1948
4. Knots Landing
5. Monty Python's Flying Circus
6. Mortimer Mouse
7. The French Connection
8. Dynasty, she played Amanda Carrington
9. Russell Crowe
10. Marilyn Monroe

ROUND 2
FILM & TV 9

QUESTIONS

1. In the hit TV show 'Dallas' what relation to Bobby Ewing was Sue Ellen?
2. What year was 'The Likely Lads' first shown?
3. On British TV what year did 'The Black and White Minstrels Show' run until?
4. Which 1970's American quiz show was hosted by Art Fleming?
5. Where was actor Russell Crowe born?
6. Which sitcom featured a father and son rag and bone business?
7. On 'The Generation Game' who was Bruce Forsythe's co-presenter and wife?
8. What is the world's longest running television drama serial?
9. What UK city was 'The Liver Birds' set in?
10. What was the address of Samantha and Darrin Stephens in the TV show 'Bewitched'?

ANSWERS

1. Sister-in-law
2. 1964
3. 1978
4. Jeopardy
5. Wellington, New Zealand
6. Steptoe and Son
7. Anthea Redfern
8. Coronation Street which has run continuously since 1960
9. Liverpool
10. 1164 Morning Glory Circle, Westport, Connecticut

ROUND 2
FILM & TV 10

QUESTIONS

1. What does the JR in JR Ewing of Dallas fame stand for?
2. What year did British comedy legend Eric Morecambe die?
3. Who were Samantha and Darrin's nosy neighbours in the TV show 'Bewitched'?
4. Who owns and runs The Kabin papershop in 'Coronation Street'?
5. Who was the thespian husband Vivien Leigh married on August 31st 1940?
6. Who did Dex Dexter marry in the TV series 'Dynasty'?
7. How many Academy Awards did the film 'Ghandi' win?
8. In 1927 what was the first film to win the Academy Award for Best Picture?
9. In 1940 which film, directed by Alfred Hitchcock won the Best Picture Oscar?
10. What was the name of the towering zombie butler in the 60's TV comedy 'The Addams Family'?

ANSWERS

1. John Ross
2. 1984
3. Gladys and Abner Kravitz
4. Rita Sullivan
5. Laurence Olivier
6. Alexis
7. Eight
8. 'Wings' a silent movie starring Clara Bow
9. Rebecca
10. Lurch

ROUND 2
FILM & TV 11

QUESTIONS

1. What year was the first episode of 'Dallas' shown?
2. What was the name of the 'Angel' played by Farah Fawcett in 'Charlie's Angels?
3. Who played Rhett Butler in the 1939 movie 'Gone with the Wind'?
4. What is the name of the oil company headed by Blake Carrington in the TV show 'Dynasty'?
5. The 1939 movie 'Gone with the Wind' won how many Oscars?
6. What fictional area of London is Eastenders set in?
7. In 1943 which film starring Humphrey Bogart won three Oscars including Best Picture?
8. Which 1991 Disney film was the first to be awarded Best Picture Oscar for an animation?
9. Which film won the Best Picture Oscar in 2000?
10. In 1919, which 18-year-old teamed up with Ub Iwerks, to produce a series of cartoons entitled "Alice in Cartoonland."?

ANSWERS

1. 1978
2. Jill Munroe
3. Clark Gable
4. Denver Carrington
5. Eight
6. Walford
7. Casablanca
8. Beauty and the Beast
9. Gladiator
10. Walt Disney

ROUND 2
FILM & TV 12

QUESTIONS

1. In the hit TV show Dallas who played Bobby Ewing's wife Pamela?
2. Which 1960s TV show's theme song began with the line "A horse is a horse of course of course and no on can talk to a horse of course..."?
3. Which actress played Jessie in UK comedy series On The Buses?
4. Who was the first presenter on Top of the Pops?
5. In 1993 which film, directed by Steven Spielberg won the Best Picture Oscar?
6. Who had a cameo role as the Cook County assessor in the last minutes of the 1980 film The Blues Brothers?
7. What was the name of the house band on The Muppet Show?
8. Which American film actress was once 'The Coppertone Girl'?
9. Who was the unseen question master in Winner Takes All?
10. Who played Lily Munster in the TV show The Munsters?

ANSWERS

1. Victoria Principal
2. Mr Ed
3. Yootha Joyce
4. Jimmy Saville
5. Schindler's List
6. Stephen Spielberg
7. Floyd and The Electric Mayhem Band
8. Jodie Foster
9. Geoffrey Wheeler
10. Yvonne DeCarlo

ROUND 2
FILM & TV 13

QUESTIONS

1. Who's first role was in the film Scudda Hoo! Scudda Hay!, first as a girl exiting a church , and then as a girl in a canoe?
2. Which silent era legend played a faded movie star of the silent era, Norma Desmond in the 1950 film Sunset Boulevard?
3. Who is Samantha's daughter in hit TV show Bewitched?
4. What was the profession of Major Anthony Nelson in the 1960's TV show I Dream of Jeannie?
5. What is the name of the actor who played Nick Cotton in Eastenders?
6. In 1988 which film, starring Tom Cruise won the Best Picture Oscar?
7. Which film has FBI trainee Clarice Starling as lead ?
8. Dan Tanna is a private detective in which US show?
9. Who was the host of Sale of the Century?
10. Which TV quiz show was most famous for a black leather executive chair?

ANSWERS

1. Marilyn Monroe
2. Gloria Swanson
3. Tabitha
4. NASA Astronaut
5. John Altman
6. Rain Man
7. The Silence of the Lambs
8. Vega$
9. Nicholas Parsons
10. Mastermind

ROUND 2
FILM & TV 14

QUESTIONS

1. Who are the Walmington-on-Sea platoon of Local Defence Volunteers better known as?
2. What year was the first Eurovision Song Contest shown on TV?
3. Who played Roj Blake in Blake 7?
4. Who took the last pictures of Marilyn Monroe during her interview with Life magazine on July 7, 1962?
5. Which character did Hollywood legend Rock Hudson play in the TV series Dynasty?
6. In 1972 which film, starring Marlon Brando won the Best Picture Oscar?
7. In 1990 who appeared on the soap opera Santa Barbara in the role of Mason Capwell?
8. Who said "I am not interested in money. I just want to be wonderful." ?
9. What is Captain T Kirk's middle name?
10. Who played Morticia in the TV series 'The Addams Family'?

ANSWERS

1. Dad's Army
2. 1956
3. Gareth Thomas
4. Allan Grant
5. Daniel Reece
6. The Godfather
7. Leonardo DiCaprio
8. Marilyn Monroe
9. Tiberius
10. Carolyn Jones

ROUND 2
FILM & TV 15

QUESTIONS

1. What character in the TV series Dallas did actor Howard Keel play?
2. Which comedy duo is associated with the song 'Bring me Sunshine'?
3. What year was the first It's A Knockout shown?
4. Who was Larry Grayson's co-host on The Generation Game?
5. Coronation Street was the brainchild of which writer?
6. Who was the creator of Come Dancing?
7. Who was the voice of Popeye the Sailor for 45 years?
8. Which is the only X-Rated film to win the Academy Awards for Best Picture and Best Director?
9. Which English actress played the second Fallon in the TV series Dynasty?
10. Which American actor was born November 11, 1974 in Los Angeles and has the middle name Wilhelm?

ANSWERS

1. Clayton Farlow
2. Morecambe and Wise
3. 1966
4. Isla St Clair
5. Tony Warren
6. Eric Morley
7. Jack Mercer
8. Midnight Cowboy' in 1969
9. Emma Samms
10. Leonardo DiCaprio

ROUND 2
FILM & TV 16

QUESTIONS

11. What was the name of the New York advertising agency where Darrin worked for in hit TV show Bewitched?

2. Who played the voice of Charlie in Charlie's Angels?

3. Who played Melanie Hamilton in the 1939 movie Gone with the Wind?

4. Who created the puppets for The Muppet Show?

5. Which of the Charlie's Angels lasted the show's five year run?

6. In 1969 which film, starring Dustin Hoffman and John Voight won the Best Picture Oscar?

7. How many academy awards did 1999 film American Beauty win?

8. In the TV show The Addams Family what or who was Cleopatra?

9. In the TV show Dallas who were the birth parents of Pam and Bobby Ewing's adopted son Christopher?

10. Which British actress is director Sam Mendes married to?

ANSWERS

1. McMann and Tate
2. Dynasty star John Forsythe
3. Olivia de Havilland
4. Jim Henson
5. Jaclyn Smith
6. Midnight Cowboy
7. Five
8. An African strangling plant
9. JR Ewing and Kristen Shepard (Sue Ellen's sister)
10. Kate Winslet

ROUND 3

MUSIC

ROUND 2
MUSIC 1

QUESTIONS

1. What year did Elvis release "That's All Right" / "Blue Moon Of Kentucky"
2. Which English composer was organist at Westminster Abbey from 1679?
3. How old was Patsy Cline when she died in a plane crash in 1963?
4. Who was the first Russian composer to establish an audience with western audiences?
5. Which dub reggae artist and producer popularized the use of the melodica?
6. Who penned "Mannish Boy," and the rock/ blues anthem "I've Got My Mojo Working"?
7. Who is the song 'Sweet Child O' Mine' by?
8. Who is the 1973 album 'Aladdin Sane' by?
9. Who wrote the 1902 opera 'Saul and David'?
10. In 1980 which band had an album titled 'Back in Black'?

ANSWERS

1. 1954
2. Henry Purcell
3. 30
4. Peter Ilyich Tchaikovsky
5. Augustus Pablo
6. Muddy Waters
7. Guns 'n' Roses
8. David Bowie
9. Carl Nielsen
10. AC/DC

ROUND 3
MUSIC 2

QUESTIONS

1. What is the name of Bob Seger's backing band?
2. Which pop group had albums titled 'Make it Big' and 'Fantastic'?
3. Who's recording debut was "Wichita Falls Blues"/"Trinity River Blues" in 1929?
4. Who produced the album 'Let it Be' for the Beatles?
5. Who was known as the Mad Monk?
6. Who composed 'Moon River'?
7. Who is the lead singer of Motorhead?
8. Which female jazz singer is the winner of thirteen Grammy Awards?
9. The Blue Moon Boys were the original backing band for who?
10. What year did Michael Jackson first perform The Moonwalk?

ANSWERS

1. The Silver Bullet Band
2. Wham
3. T-Bone Walker
4. Phil Spector
5. Thelonius Monk , jazz pianist
6. Henry Mancini
7. Lemmy (full name Lemmy Kilmister)
8. Ella Fitzgerald
9. Elvis Presley
10. 1983

ROUND 3
MUSIC 3

QUESTIONS

1. Which Rolling Stone once served in the RAF?
2. Led Zeppelin's "Whole Lotta Love" was appropriated without credit as was "You Need Love" and "You Shook Me" from which prolific blues legend?
3. Dick Dale was one of the pioneers in the 1960s of which kind of music?
4. What band did Johnny Rotten form after the Sex Pistols?
5. Who said "Before Elvis, there was nothing"
6. Who sang the theme tune to Bond film 'Goldfinger'?
7. Who is Elton John's songwriting partner?
8. Which 80's band were "too shy shy.."?
9. In the 40's and 50's who made popular songs like "Tenderly", "It's Magic" and "Sassy"?
10. What was Madonna's first single?

ANSWERS

1. Bill Wyman
2. Willie Dixon (Dixon and his publisher received credit and royalties after a lawsuit was settled out of court)
3. Surf rock
4. Public Image Ltd
5. John Lennon
6. Shirley Bassey
7. Bernie Taupin
8. Kajagoogoo
9. Ella Fitzgerald
10. Everybody

ROUND 3
MUSIC 4

QUESTIONS

1. Who was born John Michael Osbourne on December 3rd 1948 in Birmingham England?
2. Kennedy Gordy, Berry's son is better known as which Motown musician
3. Which jazz legend was born Eleanora Fagan?
4. What belt was Elvis in karate?
5. Where did The Beatles perform their last concert before paying fans?
6. Who wrote "Blue Suede Shoes" on an old potato sack in 1956?
7. Which city was host to the first performance of Mozart's opera 'The Marriage of Figaro' in 1786?
8. What was the nickname of Led Zeppelin's private jet?
9. Jackie, Tito, Jermaine, Marlon and Michael, formed which group?
10. American blues harmonica player, singer and songwriter Alex Miller, Rice Miller, Willie Williams, Willie Miller, "Little Boy Blue", "The Goat" and "Footsie," is more commonly known as whom?

ANSWERS

1. Ozzy Osbourne
2. Rockwell
3. Billie Holiday
4. A black belt
5. Candlestick Park in San Francisco, on 29 August 1966
6. Carl Perkins
7. Vienna
8. The Starship
9. The Jackson 5
10. Sonny Boy Williamson

ROUND 3
MUSIC 5

QUESTIONS

1. Which rock 'n' roll musician died in a plane crash on Feb 3rd 1959?
2. Micky Dolenz, Peter Tork, Mike Nesmith & Davy Jones are better known as who?
3. Which US city is the home of country music?
4. In the mid-50s who released "Evil" and "Smokestack Lightnin"?
5. On 25 September 1980, shortly before embarking on the U.S. leg of the tour, the drummer of Led Zeppelin died of an accidental asphyxiation after an alcohol binge. What was his name?
6. Who is the most successful group in black music history?
7. Who was Elvis's legendary manager
8. Which band had hits with 'Albatross' and 'Dreams'?
9. Who was the lead singer with The Pips?
10. "Womp-bomp-a-loom-op-a-womp-bam-boom!" is the first line of which song?

ANSWERS

1. Buddy Holly
2. The Monkees
3. Nashville
4. Howlin' Wolf
5. John Bonham
6. The Temptations having sold an estimated 22 million albums by 1982
7. Colonel Tom Parker
8. Fleetwood Mac
9. Gladys Knight
10. Tutti Frutti

ROUND 3
MUSIC 6

QUESTIONS

1. Which jazz artist's mother, Sadie Fagan, was just 13 at the time of her birth and her father was 15?
2. Which British composer wrote the War Requiem for the consecration of Coventry Cathedral in 1962?
3. Who wrote the Patsy Cline song "Crazy"?
4. Who wrote "Wang Dang Doodle"?
5. The I Threes were which reggae artists backing band?
6. What is the second biggest-selling album of all time worldwide with over 28 million copies sold?
7. What was the name of Elvis's twin brother who died?
8. Whose children are named Moon Unit, Dweezil, Ahmet Rodan and Diva?
9. Which band was originally known as Feedback?
10. Who's first-ever recording was "Your Mother's Son-In-Law" in 1933?

ANSWERS

1. Billie Holliday
2. Benjamin Britten
3. Willie Nelson
4. Willie Dixon
5. Bob Marley's after the original Wailers left
6. The Eagles, Greatest Hits (1971-1975) which has sold 28 million copies
7. Jesse Garon Presley
8. Frank Zappa
9. U2
10. Billie Holliday

ROUND 3
MUSIC 7

QUESTIONS

1. Which band has albums titled 'Bleach' and 'Nevermind'?
2. Which group was originally known as The Elgins?
3. Which Jamaican reggae legend has collaborated with Massive Attack?
4. Who are the most influential popular music group of the rock era, and the most successful, with global sales exceeding 1.3 billion records as of 2004?
5. American blues musician McKinley Morganfield is better known as whom?
6. What is the highest range of female voice?
7. Who wrote the jazz classics "Manteca", "A Night in Tunisia", "Birk's Works", and "Con Alma"?
8. Richard Wayne Penniman born December 5, 1932 in Macon, Georgia is better know as who?
9. What was Bob Marley's middle name?
10. What is Dollywood?

ANSWERS

1. Nirvana
2. The Temptations
3. Horace Andy
4. The Beatles
5. Muddy Waters
6. Soprano
7. Dizzy Gillespie
8. Little Richard
9. Nesta
10. Dolly Parton's theme park

ROUND 3
MUSIC 8

QUESTIONS

1. Which famous opera soprano singer was born Maria Anna Sofia Cecilia Kalogeropoulos?
2. What date did Nirvana frontman die?
3. Which reggae artist released 'Night Nurse' in 1982?
4. In 1935 in which US city was the first performance of Gershwin's 'Porgy and Bess'?
5. When did Elvis die?
6. What is the biggest-selling album of all time worldwide with over 50 million copies sold?
7. For most of their career, who produced The Beatles?
8. Which female jazz legend is gifted with a three-octave vocal range?
9. What year was Johan Sebastian Bach born?
10. Which German composer suffered increasing deafness from around the age of 28?

ANSWERS

1. Maria Callas
2. Friday April 8th, 1994
3. Gregory Isaacs
4. Boston
5. August 16, 1977
6. Michael Jackson's 'Thriller'
7. George Martin
8. Ella Fitzgerald
9. 1770
10. Ludwig van Beethoven

QUESTIONS

1. Which Australian soap did pop princess Kylie Minogue shoot to fame in?
2. Who sung about a 10th Avenue freeze out?
3. What is the harmonica also known as?
4. What type of jazz is played on the piano, using a repeated motif in the left hand?
5. 1951, Cleveland, Ohio disc jockey Alan Freed began playing what kind of music?
6. On April 14 2004, who was awarded the Living Legend medal by U.S. Library of Congress for her contributions to the cultural heritage of the United States?
7. The 1920 opera 'Die tote Stadt' is written by whom?
8. Reggae is generally associated with which country?
9. During World War II which British singer was known as "The Forces' Sweetheart"?
10. Which of Led Zeppelin album first featured "Whole Lotta Love"?

ANSWERS

1. Neighbours
2. Bruce Springsteen
3. A blues harp
4. Boogie-Woogie
5. Rock 'n' Roll
6. Dolly Parton
7. Eric Wolfgang Korngold
8. Jamaica
9. Vera Lynn
10. Their second album, Led Zeppelin II

ROUND 3
MUSIC 10

QUESTIONS

1. What year The Rolling Stones formed?
2. Who was born Doris Mary Ann von Kappelhoff on April 3 1924 in Evanston, Ohio?
3. In which US city was Madonna born?
4. Which legendary blues man is often called 'The King of the Mississippi Delta Blues'?
5. What was jazz often called in its early days?
6. In which US city did Motown originate?
7. 'Johnny B. Goode' was written in 1955 by whom?
8. Which country singer was married at the age of 13 and had four children by the time she was 17?
9. What is the world's best-selling music instrument?
10. Who is Don Van Vliet better known as?

ANSWERS

1. 1961
2. Doris Day
3. Michigan
4. Robert Johnson
5. Jass
6. Detroit (Motor City)
7. Chuck Berry
8. Loretta Lynn
9. The harmonica
10. Captain Beefheart

ROUND 3
MUSIC 11

QUESTIONS

1. Who wrote "It Don't Mean a Thing (If It Aint't Got That Swing)"?
2. The Rolling Stones named themselves after a song by which blues artist?
3. Who recorded "Rock Around the Clock" for Decca Records on April 12, 1954?
4. On Monday 24 February 1992 at a ceremony on Waikiki Beach, Hawaii who did Kurt Cobain marry?
5. Which Italian-American crooner's first great ambition was to be the best barber in his home town of Canonsburg, Pennsylvania?
6. What was Madonna's first number one hit?
7. Who was 'The Man in Black'?
8. Who composed the opera 'The Bartered Bride'?
9. Who wrote the 1976 opera 'Einstein on the Beach'?
10. The name of which musical genre is said to have come from the book 'Naked Lunch' by William Boroughs?

ANSWERS

1. Duke Ellington
2. Muddy Waters
3. Bill Haley and his Comets
4. Courtney Love
5. Perry Como
6. Like A Virgin
7. Johnny Cash
8. Bed ich Smetana
9. Phillip Glass
10. Heavy metal

ROUND 3
MUSIC 12

QUESTIONS

1. Which opera singer was also known as "La Divina"?
2. Who composed the 1925 opera 'Wozzeck'?
3. Who were Wham's backing band?
4. Who are Siobhan Fahey, Karen Woodward, and Sarah Dallin better known as?
5. Wall of Sound is a phrase used to describe the effect created by the music production techniques of legendary record producer?
6. Who is the lead singer of The Rolling Stones?
7. "I Left My Heart in San Francisco" was sung by which crooner?
8. Who's first band was called The Breakfast Club?
9. What instrument is John Coltrane famed for?
10. Elvis Aaron Presley was born when?

ANSWERS

1. Maria Callas
2. Alban Berg
3. Pepsi and Shirley
4. Bananarama
5. Phil Spector
6. Mick Jagger
7. Tony Bennett
8. Madonna
9. The saxophone
10. January 8, 1935

ROUND 2
MUSIC 13

QUESTIONS

1. LaVerne, Maxene and Patty were better known as which famous singing trio?
2. What is the 'Grand Ole Opry'?
3. Which 'grunge' band was founded in 1987 in Aberdeen, Washington USA?
4. Cary Grant played which composer in the film 'Night and Day'?
5. Record label Studio 1 is famous for which musical genre?
6. In 1990, the IRS gave which country singer a bill for $16.7 million in back taxes and took away most of his assets to pay off the charges?
7. At which band's free 1969 concert in Altamont, California was a fan stabbed and beaten to death by the Hell's Angels employed as security?
8. Who was the founder of Motown?
9. Which jazz artiste once destroyed an $800 bass onstage?
10. In 1979, who became part of the Patrick Hernandez Revue, a disco outfit who had the hit "Born to Be Alive"?

ANSWERS

1. The Andrews Sisters
2. A weekly Saturday night country music radio program in Nashville
3. Nirvana
4. Cole Porter
5. Reggae
6. Willy Nelson
7. The Rolling Stones
8. Berry Gordy
9. Charles Mingus
10. Madonna

ROUND 3

MUSIC 14

QUESTIONS

1. George Alan O'Dowd is better known as whom?
2. Which French composer of the romantic era entered the prestigious Paris Conservatory of Music at the unheard-of age of nine?
3. What was the name of George Gershwin's brother?
4. Who's 1973 album was titled Goats Head Soup?
5. Contrary to the belief that Michael Jackson invented The Moonwalk, who actually did?
6. Which 1980's boy band was actor Mark Wahlberg a member of?
7. Born January 29, 1885, blues legend Huddie William Ledbetter is better know as whom?
8. What was jazz saxophonist and composer Charlie Parker nicknamed?
9. In the early 1970's which Jamaican producer formed The Black Ark recording studio?
10. In 1875 which city was host to the first ever performance of Bizet's 'Carmen'?

ANSWERS

1. Boy George
2. Georges Bizet
3. Ira
4. The Rolling Stones
5. Jeffrey Daniels of Shalamar
6. New Kids on the Block
7. Leadbelly
8. Bird
9. Lee 'Scratch' Perry
10. Paris

ROUND 2
MUSIC 15

QUESTIONS

1. Who had a album titled 'Songs in the Key of Life'
2. What year did the first performance of the Verdi opera 'La Traviata' take place in Venice?
3. Who was the front man of heavy metal band Black Sabbath?
4. Which band have had more number one albums than any other group (19 in the U.S. and 15 in the United Kingdom)?
5. Which jazz singer was known as 'Lady Day'?
6. Who is Robert Allen Zimmerman better known as?
7. When was The Beach Boys 'Pet Sounds' released?
8. David Robert Jones is better known as who?
9. What is W.C. Handy's signature blues composition?
10. Which song was used by Microsoft to launch their Windows 95 operating system?

ANSWERS

1. Stevie Wonder
2. 1853
3. Ozzy Osbourne
4. The Beatles
5. Billie Holliday
6. Bob Dylan
7. May 16th 1966
8. David Bowie
9. St.Louis Blues
10. The Rolling Stones' song "Start Me Up"

ROUND 3
MUSIC 16

QUESTIONS

1. "Blowin' in the Wind" and "The Times They Are A-Changin' are songs by which artist?
2. Who wrote the classic jazz album, 'Kind of Blue'?
3. Which record label spearheaded the 1980's Ska revival?
4. Who was the lead singer with girl group The Supremes?
5. Around March 1926, who released 'Booster Blues' and 'Dry Southern Blues'?
6. "Dancing in the Street" was a 1964 hit for which group?
7. 'Fattenin' Frogs for Snakes' was made famous by which blues legend?
8. What is the most covered song in history, appearing in the Guinness Book of Records with over three thousand recorded versions.?
9. 'Natty Dread' and 'Exodus' were albums for which artist?
10. What instrument did George Harrison play in The Beatles?

ANSWERS

1. Bob Dylan
2. Miles Davis
3. 2Tone Records
4. Diana Ross
5. Blind Lemon Jefferson
6. Martha & the Vandellas
7. Sonny Boy Williamson
8. The Beatles' "Yesterday"
9. Bob Marley
10. Lead guitar

ULTIMATE BRAINBUSTER

ROUND 4
HISTORY

ROUND 4
HISTORY 1

QUESTIONS

1. How many children did Queen Victoria have?
2. Who was Ptolemy Dionysius related to as both brother and husband?
3. 21 October, 1805 is the anniversary of which famous battle?
4. Who is the father of Queen Elizabeth II?
5. In which year was the law abolished that allowed witches to be burned?
6. Great Britain was the first country to issue postage stamps, in what year?
7. The world's first travel agency was founded in 1850 by whom?
8. Calpurnia was the third wife of which Roman emperor?
9. In 1921 who founded the first birth control clinic in London?
10. What was launched in 1960 and became closely linked with the changing sexual attitudes of the 'Swinging Sixties'?

ANSWERS

1. Nine
2. Cleopatra
3. Trafalgar
4. George VI
5. 1736
6. 1840
7. Thomas Cook
8. Julius Caesar
9. Marie Stopes
10. The 'Pill'

ROUND 4
HISTORY 2

QUESTIONS

1. Which US President was forced to resign in 1974?
2. What year saw the imposition of martial law in Poland?
3. How long did the Hundred Years War last?
4. Which war involving the UK began in 1982?
5. Which architect designed the White House?
6. How long was the American Civil War?
7. What year was the General Strike?
8. Who was ousted by Corazon Aquino in 1986?
9. What year did Great Britain gain control of Hong Kong?
10. Which state became the 47th US state in 1912?

ANSWERS

1. Nixon
2. 1981
3. 116 years
4. The Falklands War
5. James Hoban
6. Four years
7. 1926
8. Ferdinand Marcos
9. 1842
10. New Mexico

ROUND 4
HISTORY 3

QUESTIONS

1. Where did the Mayflower set sail from in 1620?
2. What became America's 50th State on August 21st, 1959?
3. How many Pilgrims were aboard the Mayflower?
4. Who was the first US President to take residence in the White House?
5. What year did Mikhail Gorbachev become leader of the Soviet Union?
6. Who led a 125-mile march of child workers to President Theodore Roosevelt's vacation home on Long Island?
7. What did British Troops destroy in Washington DC in 1814?
8. What year was the Great Fire of London?
9. Which space rocket was destroyed during ground tests at Cape Canaveral in 1967?
10. Who was Henry Bolingbroke's father?

ANSWERS

1. Southampton
2. Hawaii
3. 120
4. John Adams
5. 1985
6. Mary Harris Jones
7. The President's House
8. 1666
9. Apollo 1
10. John of Gaunt – the Duke of Lancaster

ROUND 4
HISTORY 4

QUESTIONS

1. What was the colonial name of Ghana?
2. What year did India gain independence from British colonial rule?
3. How many times was Queen Elizabeth I married?
4. In 1613 who did Pocahontas marry?
5. What year was Abraham Lincoln assassinated?
6. What was the coronation year of Queen Elizabeth II?
7. In which century were the Wars of the Roses fought?
8. What did Lord Carnarvon and Howard Carter discover in 1922?
9. What year was the old-age pension introduced?
10. In 1715, Louis XIV of France was succeeded by Louis XV, what relation was he?

ANSWERS

1. Gold Coast
2. 1947
3. None
4. John Rolfe
5. 1865
6. 1952
7. The Fifteenth Century
8. The tomb of Tutankhamen
9. 1908
10. Great-grandson

ROUND 4
HISTORY 5

QUESTIONS

1. Who was the first Roman Emperor?
2. What year was the tomb of Tutankhamen discovered by Lord Carnarvon and Howard Carter?
3. What year did the Spanish Civil War begin?
4. Where in Egypt is the tomb of Tutankhamen?
5. What year did the Vietnam War begin?
6. Which king was overthrown as a result of the French Revolution?
7. What year did the French Revolution begin?
8. The Charge of the Light Brigade happened during which war?
9. What year was Queen Elizabeth I born?
10. Who was the first Christian Emperor of Rome?

ANSWERS

1. Augustus (Gaius Julius Octavianus)
2. 1922
3. 1936
4. Valley of the Kings, Luxor
5. 1954
6. Louis XVI
7. 1789
8. Crimean
9. 1533
10. Constantine the Great

ROUND 4
HISTORY 6

QUESTIONS

1. Which 1776 American affirmation asserted the basic rights of all to "life, liberty and the pursuit of happiness"?
2. Which revolution began in 1789?
3. How many days after Hiroshima did Nagasaki receive the second atom bomb?
4. When did Napoleon Bonaparte begin his reign as emperor of France?
5. Which political party rose to power in China in 1949?
6. What major event happened in Russian in 1917?
7. What year was the Berlin wall erected?
8. What year did the American Civil War end?
9. Which French ruler was finally defeated in 1815?
10. What year was the Chinese Republic established?

ANSWERS

1. American Declaration of Independence
2. The French Revolution
3. Three
4. 1804
5. The Communists
6. The Russian Revolution
7. 1961
8. 1865
9. Napoleon
10. 1911

ROUND 4
HISTORY 7

QUESTIONS

1. What year did World War I begin?
2. What year did World War I end?
3. 1970 saw which treaty between West Germany and USSR?
4. Who became the Chancellor of Germany in 1933?
5. What year was the United Nations Organisation formed?
6. In 1959 who established a communist government in Cuba?
7. What year did India gain independence, marking the start of decolonisation?
8. What year was the French Declaration of the Rights of Man (liberty, equality and fraternity)?
9. Which city did the Allies liberate on August 25th 1944?
10. In 1968 which country did USSR invade to stamp out liberal reform?

ANSWERS

1. 1914
2. 1918
3. The Moscow Treaty
4. Adolf Hitler
5. 1945
6. Fidel Castro
7. 1947
8. 1789
9. Paris
10. Czechoslovakia

ROUND 4
HISTORY 8

QUESTIONS

1. What year was the American Constitution established?
2. Which king declared himself supreme head of the Church of England?
3. What year was Long Parliament established in England?
4. Who liberated Auschwitz in January 1945?
5. Which English king was executed in 1649?
6. What is the name of the 1679 act that established freedom from arbitrary arrest in England?
7. What year was the 'Glorious Revolution?
8. What world changing event happened on September 3rd 1939?
9. What year did William of Orange land in England?
10. What year saw the union of England and Scotland?

ANSWERS

1. 1787
2. Henry VIII
3. 1640
4. Soviet troops
5. Charles I
6. Habeas Corpus Act
7. 1688
8. World War 2 began
9. 1688
10. 1707

ROUND 4
HISTORY 9

QUESTIONS

1. Japan took the British colony of Hong Kong on Christmas Day of which year?
2. The unsuccessful assassination attempt on Adolf Hitler took place on July 20th of which year?
3. London came under attack in September 1944 from which new threat?
4. What date did Germany sign their unconditional surrender?
5. Which nationality of Allied troops first begin arriving in Britain in 1942?
6. Who led the Dambuster raids of WW2?
7. Who invented the bouncing bomb?
8. The damns of which German river were the targeted by the RAF's 617 Squadron in 1943?
9. On May 26th 1940, Allied Forces begin a huge operation to rescue over 330,000 men from beaches around where?
10. Where did the D-Day landings take place?

ANSWERS

1. 1942
2. 1944
3. German V2 'doodlebug' rockets
4. May 7th 1945
5. American Troops
6. Wing Commander Guy Gibson
7. Dr Barnes Wallis
8. The Ruhr
9. Dunkirk
10. Normandy

ROUND 4
HISTORY 10

QUESTIONS

1. How high was the world's first skyscraper?
2. What was Stalin's system of slave labour camps known as?
3. How many American troops lost their lives during the Battle of the Bulge?
4. Which fascist dictator was twice decorated with the Iron Cross during WW1?
5. What year was the Contagious Diseases Act repealed?
6. Britain entered what in 1973?
7. Japan rejected what on July 28th 1945?
8. Who sent 'enemies of the people' to labour camps during what the Great Purge in USSR?
9. What was the 1928 vote for women also called?
10. Which British Prime Minister fought in the Boer War in South Africa and was later taken prisoner of war?

ANSWERS

1. 10 storeys (Home Insurance office, Chicago – built in 1885)
2. The Gulag
3. 19,000
4. Adolf Hitler
5. 1883
6. The EEC
7. The Potsdam Declaration
8. Stalin
9. The Flapper Vote
10. Churchill

ROUND 4
HISTORY 11

QUESTIONS

1. The first atomic bomb was dropped on which Japanese city?
2. What treaty was signed between the United States and the Soviet Union in 1987?
3. Which British Statesman finally retired from politics in1964?
4. Which American President was struck down by polio in 1921?
5. What year was abortion made illegal in England and Wales?
6. Which Japanese island did US Marines capture on February 23rd 1945?
7. What year was the age of consent raised to 16 in Britain?
8. Who was made General Secretary of the Communist Party in 1922?
9. What year were wives given equal rights to sue for divorce on the grounds of adultery?
10. What year did Hitler become Germany's Chancellor?

ANSWERS

1. Hiroshima
2. Intermediate Nuclear Forces Treaty
3. Winston Churchill
4. Franklin D Roosevelt
5. 1803
6. Iwo Jima
7. 1885
8. Josef Stalin
9. 1923
10. 1933

ROUND 4
HISTORY 12

QUESTIONS

1. What was the British royal family's surname before they changed it to Windsor in 1917?
2. On which street did the Great Fire of London start?
3. Which Roman commander landed on the South Coast of England in 43 AD?
4. Who usurped King Richard II in 1399?
5. What year was the Channel Tunnel completed?
6. What natural product was the cornerstone of England's foreign trade in the 14th Century?
7. Which British King renounced his German titles during WWI?
8. What year was slave trading abolished in Great Britain and Ireland?
9. Which religious group was most vocal in their opposition to slave trading in the early 18th Century?
10. Who was the first Englishman to circumnavigate the globe between 1577-1580?

ANSWERS

1. Saxe-Coburg-Gotha
2. Pudding Lane
3. Aulus Plautius
4. Henry Bolingbroke
5. 1994
6. Wool
7. George V
8. 1807
9. The Quakers
10. Sir Francis Drake

ROUND 4
HISTORY 13

QUESTIONS

1. What was Sir Francis Drake's most celebrated boat called?
2. In 1614 John Rolfe married which Native American woman?
3. Who died on April 12th 1945 - less than a month before Nazi Germany surrendered?
4. What year did rationing finally end in Britain?
5. What year did Winston Churchill first take a seat in the House of Commons?
6. What year was the Boston Tea Party?
7. How long did the Romans occupy Britain?
8. What year was the Patriot Act passed in the United States?
9. What book was first compiled in 1086?
10. Which British king ruled between 1189 – 99?

ANSWERS

1. The Golden Hind
2. Pocahontas
3. Franklin D Roosevelt
4. 1954
5. 1900
6. 1773
7. 400 years
8. 2001
9. The Doomsday Book
10. Richard The Lionheart

ROUND 4
HISTORY 14

QUESTIONS

1. What was Byzantium renamed in 330 AD?
2. Albert the Great, King of Wessex, defeated who at the battle of Edington?
3. What date in 1945 did Adolf Hitler kill himself as Russian Army closed in on Berlin?
4. What year did the Butler Education Act introduce free secondary education for all?
5. What year was Churchill made Chancellor of the Exchequer?
6. Which famous battle took place in 1066?
7. What does Ghengis Khan mean?
8. What date in August 1945 did Japan surrender to finally end World War 2?
9. In 1215 what did King John I sign?
10. Who was born Iosif Vissarionovich Dzhugashvili?

ANSWERS

1. Constantinople
2. The Danes
3. April 30th
4. 1944
5. 1924
6. The Battle of Hastings
7. Supreme King
8. 14th
9. The Magna Carta
10. Josef Stalin

ROUND 4
HISTORY 15

QUESTIONS

1. What date did Germany invade Poland?
2. What year was food rationing first introduced in Britain?
3. What commenced on June 6th 1944?
4. Who replaced Neville Chamberlain as British Prime Minister in May 1940?
5. During WW2 where was the Battle of Monte Cassino?
6. The Warsaw Uprising began on August 1st of which year?
7. What date did Germany invade France?
8. Which British Navy ship was sunk by the German battleship Bismarck on May 24th, 1941?
9. In the German occupied territories of 1940, a yellow Star of David had to be worn by all Jews over what age?
10. What year did Japan attack Pearl Harbour?

ANSWERS

1. September 1st 1939
2. 1940
3. D-Day
4. Winston Churchill
5. Central Italy
6. 1944
7. May 13th, 1940
8. HMS Hood
9. Six
10. 1941

ROUND 4
HISTORY 16

QUESTIONS

1. What year was the steam engine invented?
2. Which British Prime Minister was criticized before being ousted for his appeasement of Nazi Germany?
3. Who became Archbishop of York in 1514?
4. Which Scottish king became King of England in 1603?
5. Who founded the Independent Labour Party in 1893?
6. What year was the Wall Street Crash?
7. What year was the first Roman invasion of Britain?
8. Who was Edward II's chancellor and later appointed Archbishop of Canterbury?
9. What year was the Treaty of Falaise signed?
10. Who was the first king of all England?

ANSWERS

1. 1774
2. Neville Chamberlain
3. Cardinal Wolsey
4. James VI
5. Keir Hardie
6. 1929
7. 55BC
8. Thomas Becket
9. 1174
10. Athelstan

ROUND 4
HISTORY 17

QUESTIONS

1. Florence Nightingale is associated with which war?
2. What year did the American Civil War begin?
3. Queen Elizabeth I is the daughter of Henry VIII and which of his many wives?
4. What year was the Emancipation Proclamation, issued by Abraham Lincoln?
5. Which major conflict ended in 1918?
6. What year did World War Two begin?
7. What year did the Falklands War begin?
8. Which dynasty did Henry VIII belong to?
9. What is the pseudonym of the Marxist leader Vladimir Ilich Ulyanov?
10. Fidel Castro is the prime minister of which country?

ANSWERS

1. Crimean
2. 1861
3. Anne Boleyn
4. 1863
5. World War One
6. 1939
7. 1982
8. House of Tudor
9. Lenin
10. Cuba

ROUND 4
HISTORY 18

QUESTIONS

1. What was the name of the son of Cleopatra and Julius Ceasar?
2. Who became the first female science lecturer at Manchester University in 1904?
3. What year did Edward VIII abdicate?
4. In 1912, US Army Captain Albert Berry was the first to do what?
5. Which of Henry VIII's wives survived him?
6. In which year did the US launch a male chimpanzee called Ham into space?
7. How long was Queen Victoria's reign?
8. What year did Jamaica gain independence from British colonial rule?
9. Which dynasty did Elizabeth I belong to?
10. According to Pharaonic custom, which Egyptian Queen was married to her brother?

ANSWERS

1. Caesarion
2. Marie Stopes
3. 1936
4. Make the first parachute jump from a moving airplane
5. Catherine Parr
6. 1969
7. 64 years
8. 1962
9. House of Stuart
10. Cleopatra

ROUND 5
POLITICS

ROUND 5
POLITICS 1

QUESTIONS

1. Which political party is Jeffrey Archer associated with?
2. Who is the longest serving Australian Prime Minister?
3. What does WSPU stand for?
4. What year was Malcolm X assassinated?
5. Which political party is Virginia Bottomley associated with?
6. In which year was the law passed giving women over 30 the right to vote in parliamentary elections?
7. What system allowed the white minority but disallowed the black and coloured majority of South Africa to vote?
8. During the 1930's and 40's in Nazi Germany, Jews and Gypsies were forced to wear what colour ribbons?
9. Which black activist was born Malcolm Little in Omaha, Nebraska on May 19th 1925?
10. Which US President signed the Voting Rights Act into law on August 6, 1965?

ANSWERS

1. Conservative
2. Robert Menzies
3. The Women's Social and Political Union
4. 1965
5. Conservative
6. 1918
7. Apartheid
8. Yellow
9. Malcolm X
10. Lyndon B. Johnson

ROUND 5
POLITICS 2

QUESTIONS

1. Which political party's 2005 manifesto used the words 'Britain forward not back'?
2. Who leads the labour party in Scotland?
3. Who leads the labour party in Wales?
4. Which political party is Dianne Abbott associated with?
5. What was Winston Churchill's full name?
6. What is the profession of Tony Blair's wife Cherie?
7. Which political group adopted purple, white and green as it's official colours?
8. Which political party is Kenneth Baker associated with?
9. Which political party is Petrina Holdsworth associated with?
10. In 1955 The Montgomery Bus Boycott was lead by which famous black civil rights activist?

ANSWERS

1. Labour
2. Jack McConnell
3. Rhodri Morgan
4. Labour
5. Winston Leonard Spencer
6. Lawyer
7. Suffragettes
8. Conservative
9. The United Kingdom Independence Party
10. Martin Luther King Jr

ROUND 5
POLITICS 3

QUESTIONS

1. Which Indian Prime Minister was assassinated in October 1984?
2. Mahatma Ghandi was assassinated by a Hindu nationalist in which year?
3. What is the middle name of John F Kennedy?
4. Which political party is Edward Davey associated with?
5. Who is the author of 'Mein Kampf'?
6. Who renounced his peerage (as 14th Earl of Home) to fight (and lose) the general election of 1964?
7. Which political party is Stephen Byers associated with?
8. What year was John F Kennedy assassinated?
9. What nationality is Labour politician Neil Kinnock?
10. Which political party is Peter Lilley associated with?

ANSWERS

1. Indira Gandhi
2. 1948
3. Fitzgerald
4. Liberal Democrat
5. Adolf Hitler
6. Sir Alec Douglas Home
7. Labour
8. 1963
9. Welsh
10. Conservative

ROUND 5
POLITICS 4

QUESTIONS

1. Which political party is Mark Oaten associated with?
2. Which political party is Charles Clark associated with?
3. Which political party is John Gummer associated with?
4. Who was the first female leader of a Muslim state?
5. Who was the US President before Ronald Reagan?
6. Who was the 34th President of the United States?
7. In which US city was John F Kennedy assassinated?
8. What country was Adolf Hitler born?
9. Who was the youngest person to be
elected President of the United States?
10. Which political party is Roger Knapman associated with?

1. Liberal Democrat
2. Labour
3. Conservative
4. Benazir Bhutto
5. James Earl Carter
6. Dwight D Eisenhower
7. Dallas
8. Austria
9. John F Kennedy
10. The United Kingdom Independence Party

ROUND 5
POLITICS 5

QUESTIONS

1. Which political party is Nigel Lawson associated with?
2. Who was Education Secretary from 1970 to 1974 in Edward Heath's government?
3. Who succeeded Neville Chamberlain as Prime Minister?
4. How many times was Harold Wilson Prime Minister?
5. Which British Prime Minister was born in Grantham, England on 13th October 1925?
6. In 1922, who succeeded David Lloyd George as Prime Minister?
7. Which political leader was born Margaret Hilda Roberts?
8. Who preceded John Howard as Australian Prime Minister?
9. Which political party is Gordon Brown associated with?
10. Which political party is Diana Maddock associated with?

ANSWERS

1. Conservative
2. Margaret Thatcher
3. Winston Churchill
4. Twice, 1964-70 then 1974-76
5. Margaret Thatcher
6. Andrew Bonar Law
7. Margaret Thatcher
8. Bob Hawke
9. Labour
10. Liberal Democrat

ROUND 5
POLITICS 6

QUESTIONS

1. What is the middle name of former British Prime Minister Margaret Thatcher?
2. Which Russian revolutionary was assassinated in Mexico with an ice pick?
3. Which Polish trade-union leader founded Solidarity in 1980?
4. What was the name of Adolf Hitler's mistress?
5. In which London borough is 10 Downing Street situated?
6. What year did The Wall Street crash happen in America?
7. Number 10 Downing Street is home to the Prime Minister, who lives at number 11?
8. Who was the first woman M.P. to have a seat in the House of Commons?
9. What was the adopted name of Polish revolutionary Lev Davidovitch Bronstein?
10. Which Polish trade-union leader won the Nobel Peace Prize in 1983?

ANSWERS

1. Hilda
2. Leon Trotsky
3. Lech Walesa
4. Eva Braun
5. Westminster
6. 1929
7. The Chancellor of the Exchequer
8. Viscountess (Nancy) Astor
9. Leon Trotsky
10. Lech Walesa

ROUND 5
POLITICS 7

QUESTIONS

1. Screaming Lord Sutch or Lord David Sutch was the leader of which political party?
2. Which political party is Kenneth Clarke associated with?
3. Which political party is Charles Kennedy associated with?
4. What name is given to the Ministers in the Scottish Parliament?
5. What date was Tony Blair elected Prime Minister?
6. What year was the labour party founded?
7. Keir Hardy was the first leader of which political party from 1906-1908?
8. Who was the leader of the labour party prior to Tony Blair?
9. Which political party is Tony Banks associated with?
10. Who was the leader of the Labour Party in 1981?

ANSWERS

1. The Monster Raving Looney Party
2. Conservative
3. Liberal Democrat
4. The Executive
5. May 2nd 1997
6. 1900
7. The Labour Party
8. John Smith
9. Labour
10. Michael Foot

ROUND 5
POLITICS 8

QUESTIONS

1. Which political party is Paul Boateng associated with?
2. What year did the Burundi-Rwanda civil war end?
3. Which US President wrote his own epitaph without mentioning that he was US President?
4. In UK politics, under the Blair government who was 2001 Foreign Secretary?
5. In 2001 who was forced to resign from his position as Northern Ireland Secretary due to a naturalization scandal?
6. Who became Health Secretary in 2003?
7. On August 18, 1920 the 19th amendment to the U.S. Constitution was ratified and granted women the right to do what?
8. Which political party is John Gummer associated with?
9. Who was the Trade and Industry Secretary from 1998-1999?
10. Which political party is Jeffrey Archer associated with?

ANSWERS

1. Labour
2. 2000
3. Thomas Jefferson
4. Jack Straw
5. Peter Mandelson
6. Dr John Reid
7. Vote
8. Conservative
9. Peter Mandelson
10. Conservative

QUESTIONS

1. Which political party is Betty Boothroyd associated with?
2. Which political party is Nigel Lawson associated with?
3. What does UKIP stand for?
4. What year was Nelson Mandela incarcerated?
5. What does ANC stand for?
6. Michael Manley was prime minister of which country?
7. Which fascist dictator led Italy into World War II in support of Hitler?
8. … what year was this dictator killed?
9. Which political party is Paddy Ashdown associated with?
10. Which US President resigned in 1974 after being threatened with impeachment?

ANSWERS

1. Labour
2. Conservative
3. The United Kingdom Independence Party
4. 1964
5. African National Congress
6. Jamaica
7. Benito Mussolini
8. 1945
9. Liberal Democrat
10. Richard Nixon

ROUND 5
POLITICS 10

QUESTIONS

1. Which US President was given the nickname 'Tricky Dicky'?
2. Which country was Pinochet military ruler of from 1973?
3. Which US President was a former Hollywood actor?
4. What year was Ronald Reagan elected US President?
5. Which US President launched the New Deal economic and social reform programme during the Depression?
6. What is the middle name of former US President Richard Nixon?
7. Who was the Portuguese prime minister form 1932-68?
8. Who is the Soviet politician Joseph Vissarionovich Djugashvili better known as?
9. Which US President is famous for his involvement in the Watergate scandal?
10. Who was president of the African National Congress from 1977?

ANSWERS

1. Richard Nixon
2. Chile
3. Ronald Reagan
4. 1981
5. Franklin D Roosevelt
6. Milhous
7. Antonio de Oliveira Salazar
8. Stalin
9. Richard Nixon
10. Oliver Tambo

ROUND 5
POLITICS 11

QUESTIONS

1. What do the initial EMU stand for?
2. What would a paid official responsible to the Crown be otherwise know as?
3. Who was the first woman to run for office of US President?
4. What year was The United Nations organisation (UN) founded?
5. The European Union was founded in 1957 as what?
6. Where was George Washington inaugurated for his first term, on 30 April 1789?
7. Where did George Washington's second inauguration take place?
8. Who was the first US President to be inaugurated in Washington DC?
9. Who had the shortest term of office as US President, serving for 32 days, from 4 March to 4 April 1841?
10. Who had the longest term of office of 12 years?

ANSWERS

1. European Montetary Union
2. A civil servant
3. Victoria Woodhull (1838-1927)
4. 1945
5. The European Economic Community (EEC)
6. Federal Hall in New York City.
7. Philadelphia
8. Thomas Jefferson
9. William Henry Harrison
10. Franklin D. Roosevelt

ROUND 5
POLITICS 12

QUESTIONS

1. What is the middle name of Franklin D Roosevelt?
2. Which political party is Sir Walter Menzies Campbell associated with?
3. Who was the first President of the United States?
4. What year did George Washington take office as President of the United States?
5. Who was the President of the United States in 1950?
6. Which political party is Michael Foot associated with?
7. Which British Labour politician inaugurated the National Health Service?
8. Which former US President was director of the Central Intelligence Agency (CIA) from 1976-81?
9. Benazir Bhutto was the leader of which political party?
10. Which political party is Frances Davidson associated with?

ANSWERS

1. Delano
2. Liberal Democrat
3. George Washington
4. 1789
5. Harry S Truman
6. Labour
7. Aneurin Bevan
8. George Bush (Senior)
9. Pakistan People's Party (PPP)
10. Conservative

ROUND 5
POLITICS 13

QUESTIONS

1. Who assumed the presidency following the resignation of Richard Nixon?
2. Which US Presidential candidate had the highest popular vote ever?
3. What is the shortest war on record?
4. During the Battle of Waterloo, who had his horse shot from under him 9 times?
5. What was Chevy Chase?
6. Who is the two-finger V for Victory sign synonymous with?
7. During the French and Indian wars in North America (1689-1763), blankets used by smallpox victims were given to whom?
8. Which war has resulted in the most casualties?
9. What year did the Korean War end?
10. What year did the Vietnam War end?

ANSWERS

1. Gerald Ford
2. Ronald Reagan
3. In 1896 Zanzibar surrendered to Britain after 38 minutes
4. Lord Uxbridge
5. A battle that took place on the English-Scottish border in 1388
6. Winston Churchill
7. American Indians in the hope they would carry the disease.
8. The Second World War with 20 million casualties
9. 1953
10. 1973

ROUND 5
POLITICS 14

QUESTIONS

1. Who preceded Clement Attlee as Prime Minister?
2. Who was Tony Blair preceded by as Prime Minister?
3. Who was the leader of the Labour Party during World War II?
4. When Labour came into power in 1997 how many consecutive years had Conservative been in Government?
5. Which Labour leader once sang and played guitar in a rock band called 'The Ugly Rumours'?
6. Who married Cherie Booth on 29th March 1980?
7. Which famous Coronation Street star helped PM Tony Blair on his campaign trail?
8. Who were the other candidates when Tony Blair ran for Labour Party leader?
9. Who was Margaret Thatcher preceded by as Prime Minister?
10. Who preceded Sir Anthony Eden as Prime Minister?

ANSWERS

1. Winston Churchill
2. John Major
3. Clement Attlee 1935-1955
4. 18 years
5. PM Tony Blair
6. PM Tony Blair
7. Pat Phoenix, otherwise know as Coronation Street's Elsie Tanner who was the girlfriend of his father-in-law, Anthony Booth
8. John Prescott and Margaret Beckett
9. James Callaghan
10. Winston Churchill, his

ROUND 5
POLITICS 15

QUESTIONS

1. Which political party is Leon Brittan associated with?
2. In 1955 The Montgomery Bus Boycott was precipitated by which woman's refusal to give up her bus seat in favour of a white passenger?
3. In the United States what year was the Voting Rights Act passed?
4. Which Suffragette was famously trampled to death by the King's horse at the Epsom Derby in 1913 as she attempted a political protest?
5. Which political party is Clare Short associated with?
6. Which political party is Mike Nattrass associated with?
7. Who is the term 'By any means necessary' attributed to?
8. Which political party is Nancy Astor associated with?
9. What does SNP stand for?
10. What year did the system of Apartheid come to an end in South Africa?

ANSWERS

1. Conservative
2. Rosa Parks
3. 1965
4. Emily Davison
5. Labour
6. The United Kingdom Independence Party
7. Malcolm X
8. Conservative
9. Scottish National Party
10. 1994

ROUND 5
POLITICS 16

QUESTIONS

1. What year were women in Britain granted complete equality with men and were allowed to vote at the age of 21?
2. Which political party is John Whittaker associated with?
3. Which political party is Peter Lilley associated with?
4. Which political party is Dianne Abbott associated with?
5. What is the traditional emblem of the Labour Party?
6. Which political campaign group's motto was 'Deeds Not Words!'?
7. Which political party is Paul Burstow associated with?
8. Who did Margaret Thatcher succeed as Prime Minister in 1979?
9. What year was John Major elected Prime Minister?
10. Who replaced Clement Attlee as Prime Minister in 1951?

ANSWERS

1. 1928
2. The United Kingdom Independence Party
3. Conservative
4. Labour
5. A red rose
6. The Suffragettes
7. Liberal Democrat
8. James Callaghan
9. 1990
10. Sir Winston Churchill

ROUND 5
POLITICS 17

QUESTIONS

1. What year was Winston Churchill born?
2. Who was the first British Prime Minister?
3. What year was Margaret Thatcher elected prime minister?
4. What year was Winston Churchill elected prime minister for a second time?
5. Who replaced Harold Wilson as Prime Minister in 1976?
6. What does NATO stand for?
7. Who was President of The United States during World War II?
8. Which political party is Dr Vincent Cable associated with?
9. Which political party is Barbara Castle associated with?
10. Which political party is Stephen Dorrell associated with?

ANSWERS

1. 1874
2. Sir Robert Walpole
3. 1979
4. 1951
5. James Callahan
6. North Atlantic Treaty Organisation
7. Franklin D Roosevelt
8. Liberal Democrat
9. Labour
10. Conservative

ROUND 5
POLITICS 18

QUESTIONS

1. Which political party is Emma Nicholson associated with?
2. In 1869 which US Territory was the first to give women the right to vote?
3. Which political party is Virginia Bottomley associated with?
4. In 1872 which woman suffragette was arrested, jailed and fined for illegally voting in a National Presidential election in Rochester, New York?
5. In 1903 in Manchester, England which Suffragette founded and led the 'Woman's Social and Political Union' (WSPU)?
6. Who was nicknamed 'The Iron Lady'?
7. What is Paddy Ashdown's real first name?
8. Who abdicated his inherited peerage as Viscount Stansgate in order to remain a labour MP?
9. Who was the leader of The Monster Raving Looney Party?
10. Which political party is David Blunkett associated with?

ANSWERS

1. Liberal Democrat
2. Wyoming territory
3. Conservative
4. Susan B. Anthony
5. Emily Pankhurst
6. Margaret Thatcher
7. Jeremy
8. Tony Benn
9. Screaming Lord Sutch
10. Labour

ULTIMATE BRAINBUSTER

ROUND 6

CARS, PLANES

BOATS & TRAINS

ROUND 6

CARS, PLANES, BOATS & TRAINS 1

QUESTIONS

1. Who was the first pilot to break the sound barrier?
2. How many engines did Concorde use to achieve supersonic speed?
3. Who produces the metal rails used on train tracks in Britain?
4. Which aircraft was the first to break the sound barrier?
5. Which aircraft saw the most combat during the first Gulf War?
6. How long is the M1 motorway?
7. What is the combat range of the US Air Force B-52 Stratofortress?
8. Which WW2 German rocket scientist became a director of NASA?
9. Which was the first steam ship to cross the Atlantic?
10. Which was the first propeller-driven Atlantic crossing?

ANSWERS

1. Chuck Yeager
2. Four
3. British Steel at its plant in Workington, Cumbria
4. Bell X-1
5. F-16 Falcon
6. 187 miles
7. 14,080km
8. Werner Von Braun
9. Savannah
10. SS Great Britain

ROUND 6

CARS, PLANES, BOATS & TRAINS 2

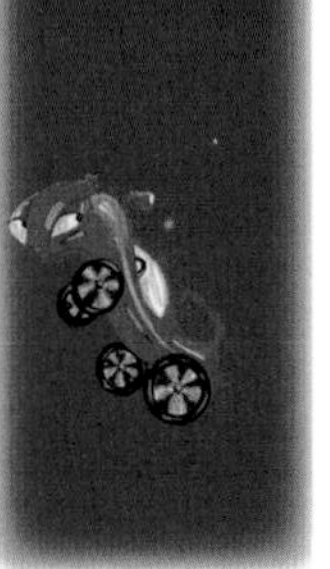

QUESTIONS

1. What was the name of the first nuclear powered boat?
2. What year war the M1 motorway first opened?
3. Which German engineer invented the diesel engine in 1892?
4. Who won the world's first motor race?
5. The world's first motor race in 1895 ran between Paris and which French city?
6. What year was the first B-2 stealth bomber was publicly unveiled at Palmdale Air Force Base in California ?
7. Pneumatic tyres were originally developed for which mode of transport?
8. What year was the first electric car introduced?
9. The shortest scheduled airline flight is made between the island of Westray to Papa Westray off Scotland. How long does it take?
10. When was the first in-flight lavatory introduced?

ANSWERS

1. Lenin
2. 1959
3. Rudolf Diesel
4. Emile Levassor
5. Bordeaux
6. 1988
7. Bicycles
8. 1896
9. 2 minutes
10. 1913

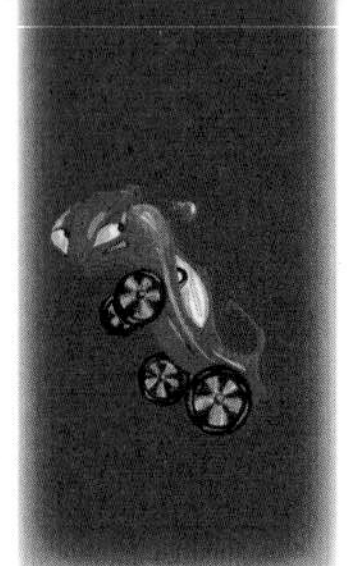

ROUND 6

CARS, PLANES, BOATS & TRAINS 3

QUESTIONS

1. How many aircraft are in the US Air Force fleet?
2. Where is Ferrari based?
3. What was Concorde's cruising speed?
4. The Channel Tunnel cost how many more times more than the Golden Gate Bridge?
5. How many times more powerful is the OOCL Shenzhen container ship than a family car?
6. How many tonnes of fuel per hour does it take to power the OOCL Shenzhen?
7. What year were the first sleeper carriages introduced on trains?
8. What year did George Mortimer Pullman produce his first luxury carriage?
9. What year was the Orient Express founded?
10. Which English train station was used as a location set for the movie, Brief Encounter?

ANSWERS

1. 15,000
2. Maranello, Italy
3. 1350mph
4. 700
5. 1,000
6. Ten
7. 1870
8. 1864
9. 1883
10. Carnforth

ROUND 6
CARS, PLANES, BOATS & TRAINS 4

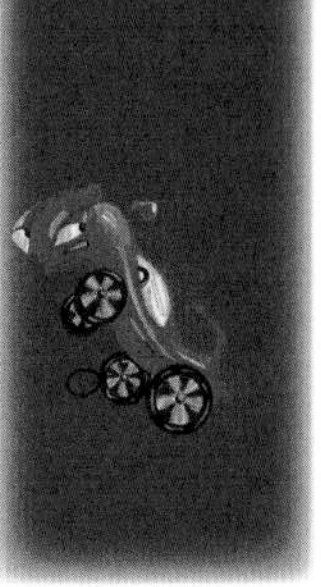

QUESTIONS

1. What percentage of all journeys does car travel account for in Britain?
2. The US government's top secret aircraft developments are collectively known by what codename?
3. The landspeed record holder, Thrust SSC, has the equivalent power of how many formula one cars?
4. What year did the McLaren F1 cease production?
5. How many McLaren F1 cars were manufactured?
6. What year did Jeremy Clarkson first present Top Gear?
7. What year was wrought iron first used for rail tracks?
8. In the Hatfield disaster of 2000, the express train was travelling between London and which other city?
9. The first railway, Liverpool & Manchester Railway, opened to the public in which year?
10. Which subway has more stations than any other in the world?

ANSWERS

1. 70%
2. Black Projects
3. 145
4. 1998
5. 106
6. 1989
7. 1820
8. Leeds
9. 1830
10. The New York City subway

ROUND 6

CARS, PLANES, BOATS & TRAINS 5

QUESTIONS

1. What year did the Spitfire enter into service with the Royal Air Force?
2. Which train station has the most platforms?
3. What year did the RAF shelve their famous Spitfire fighter?
4. Radar was first used during which famous battle?
5. What bird of prey did the RAF cull during WW2 to stop them killing their carrier pigeons?
6. What was the first ever Ferrari model?
7. Which airport lays claim to being the longest building on earth?
8. How many tones of freight is transported by rail every day in Britain?
9. What year did Heathrow airport handle its first passenger flight?
10. Approximately how many flights does Heathrow handle on an average day?

ANSWERS

1. 1938
2. Grand Central in New York
3. 1954
4. Battle of Britain
5. Peregrine Falcons
6. The Ferrari 125s
7. Kensai
8. 400,000 tones
9. 1946
10. 1,000

ROUND 6

CARS, PLANES, BOATS & TRAINS 6

QUESTIONS

1. The Ancient Egyptians built boats from what?
2. Which ancient culture developed the wooden plank-built boat?
3. The world's earliest known plank-built ship, made from cedar and sycamore wood dates back to when?
4. When did the Ancient Egyptians create their first navy?
5. Which ancient civilizations developed oar-powered ships?
6. When did oar-powered ships first appear?
7. Which civilization developed sails to power their boats?
8. Approximately when did the first sailboats appear?
9. What was the top speed of the world's first train?
10. What percentage of all journeys does rail travel account for in Britain?

ANSWERS

1. Papyrus
2. Egypt
3. 2600 BC
4. 2300 BC.
5. Sumerians
6. 3500 BC.
7. Phoenicians
8. 2000 BC
9. 8 km/h (5 mph)
10. 12%

ROUND 6
CARS, PLANES, BOATS & TRAINS 7

QUESTIONS

1. What year did the London Underground open?
2. Who built the first steam locomotive?
3. Herbie, the star of The Love Bug was what kind of car?
4. What car did Steve McQueen drive in the famous car chase in the movie, Bullitt?
5. Who designed the Mini?
6. What year was the Mini debuted?
7. What year was the Hatfield rail crash?
8. What year was the world's first public passenger railway was built?
9. Which towns did the world's first passenger train run between?
10. What year was the Paddington rail crash?

ANSWERS

1. 1863
2. Richard Trevithick
3. Volkswagen Beetle
4. Ford Mustang 390GT
5. Sir Alec Issigonis
6. 1959
7. 2000
8. 1826
9. Stockton and Darlington
10. 1999

ROUND 6

CARS, PLANES, BOATS & TRAINS 8

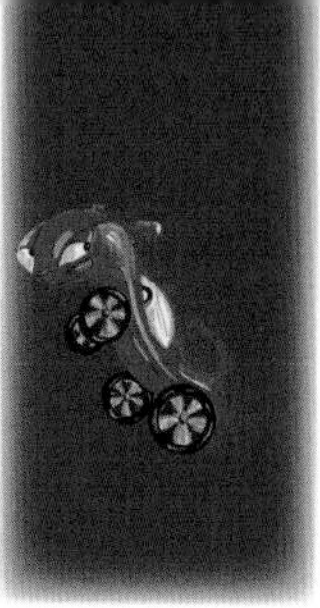

QUESTIONS

1. The world's oldest dugout canoe dates back to when?
2. What year did Dutch inventor Cornelius van Drebbel test his prototype submarine in the Thames?
3. Which country first developed speedway racing?
4. What year did the first speedway race take place?
5. The island of Manhattan has approximately how many parking meters?
6. What is the average traffic speed in Manhattan?
7. What engines did the Ford cars use?
8. Who produced America's first successful gasoline-powered automobile?
9. What year did the Duryea brothers develop their prototype gasoline car?
10. Which country was the world's oldest dugout canoe found?

ANSWERS

1. 7400BC
2. 1620
3. Australia
4. 1925
5. 16,000
6. 6.2 mph
7. Dodge
8. Duryea brothers
9. 1896
10. Netherlands

ROUND 6
CARS, PLANES, BOATS & TRAINS 9

QUESTIONS

1. How many stations does the London Underground have?
2. What year was the Ford Motor Company founded?
3. Which is the oldest metropolitan underground network in the world?
4. The Mini Cooper S won the Monte Carlo Rally for how many consecutive years?
5. Who designed the London Underground logo in 1913?
6. When was smoking banned on the London Underground?
7. Who hosts hit TV motoring show 'Top Gear'?
8. How many stations are there on New York City's Subway?
9. What year was automatic signalling introduced on the London and South Western Railway?
10. How many houses were demolished to build St. Pancras station?

ANSWERS

1. 275
2. 1903
3. London Underground
4. Four
5. Edward Johnston
6. July 1984.
7. Jeremy Clarkson
8. 468
9. 1902
10. 4,000

ROUND 6

CARS, PLANES, BOATS & TRAINS 10

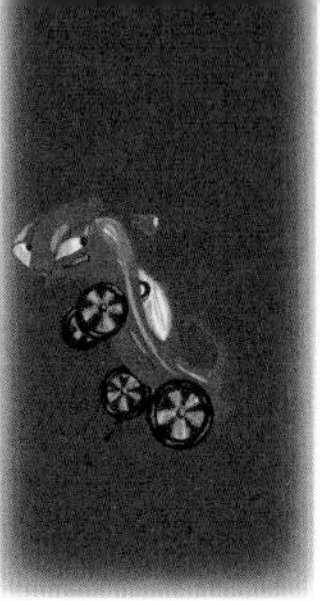

QUESTIONS

1. What percentage of the world's Boeing 747's pass through Heathrow every day?
2. How much does each B-2 stealth bomber cost?
3. In 1946, Heathrow's first passenger flight to Buenos Aires took how long to reach its destination?
4. What year did I.K. Brunel's Great Western Railway open?
5. The B-52 was crewed by how many men?
6. In1845, which railway magnate owned 33% of Britain's entire railway system?
7. Approximately how many in-flight meals are served around the world every day?
8. How many people are employed directly in the aviation industry?
9. What year did the World's first underground city railway opens in London – now known as the Metropolitan Line?
10. How many passengers did Heathrow handle in its first year?

ANSWERS

1. 10%
2. $2billion
3. 35 hours
4. 1838
5. Five
6. George Hudson
7. 4.5 million
8. 180,000
9. 1863
10. 60,000

ROUND 6
CARS, PLANES, BOATS & TRAINS 11

QUESTIONS

1. What engines were used to power Concorde?
2. What years was the first round-the-world flight?
3. In which year did Floyd Bennett and Richard Byrd make the first flight over the North Pole?
4. What year was the first non-stop Atlantic aircraft crossing?
5. What year was the Space Shuttle Columbia launched?
6. Who made the first non-stop solo flight across the Atlantic?
7. Who was the first woman to make a solo Atlantic crossing?
8. What year was the first successful solo round-the-world flight?
9. The world's oldest electric passenger train service – Volks Electric Railway - exists in which English seaside town?
10. How many people in Britain travel by rail every day?

ANSWERS

1. Rolls Royce Olympus 593
2. 1924
3. 1926
4. 1919
5. 1981
6. Charles Lindbergh
7. Amelia Earhart
8. 1933
9. Brighton
10. 2.5m

ROUND 6

CARS, PLANES, BOATS & TRAINS 12

QUESTIONS

1. What year did Thomas Newcomen invent the steam engine?
2. Which Russian bomber was a direct copy of the Boeing B-29?
3. What is Lockheed's experimental design workshop better know as?
4. Before the privatisation 1993, British Rail had been state-owned since when?
5. What year was the Southall rail crash?
6. In 1994, a law was passed where all trucks over 7 1/2 tonnes had to be mechanically restricted to what speed?
7. What does BRB stand for?
8. What year were the first Turnpike roads built?
9. How long did the first non-stop Atlantic aircraft crossing take?
10. What year were the first metal rails for train tracks produced in South Wales from cast iron?

ANSWERS

1. 1705
2. TU-4
3. Skunk Works
4. January 1st 1948
5. 1997
6. 56mph
7. British Railways Board
8. 1730s
9. 16 hours
10. 1791

ROUND 6
CARS, PLANES, BOATS & TRAINS 13

QUESTIONS

1. Where was the first Road Traffic Death?
2. What year did the Ford Motor Company fit their factory with the first moving assembly lines?
3. How many Model Ts had been manufactured by 1927?
4. How long did it take Ford production line workers to assemble a car in 1927?
5. Who invented the electric ignition and starter motor?
6. What name is the London Underground also know as?
7. What year were emissions regulations introduced in the US?
8. Controls on harmful emissions were initially introduced in which US State?
9. What year did the Arab oil embargo send oil prices rocketing?
10. Which German company developed the first antilock braking systems (ABS)?

ANSWERS

1. Crystal Palace in London
2. 1913
3. 15 million
4. 93 minutes
5. Charles Kettering
6. The Tube
7. 1965
8. California.
9. 1973
10. Bosch

ROUND 6

CARS, PLANES, BOATS & TRAINS 14

QUESTIONS

1. How many people were killed in the Hatfield train crash of October, 2000?
2. Concorde crossed the Atlantic at what altitude?
3. What year were the first metal rails used on train tracks?
4. How large is the crew of a B-2 stealth bomber?
5. Who designed the DeLorean DMC 12?
6. How many platforms does Grand Central Station in New York have?
7. Who designed St Pancras Station in London?
8. Stephenson's Rocket triumphed at the Rainhill Trials in which year?
9. Who designed the Supermarine Spitfire?
10. Which motor company was the first to increase productivity with an assembly line?

ANSWERS

1. Four
2. 60,000 ft
3. 1791
4. Two
5. Giorgetto Giugiar
6. 44
7. Sir George Gilbert Scott
8. 1829
9. Reginald Mitchell
10. Ford

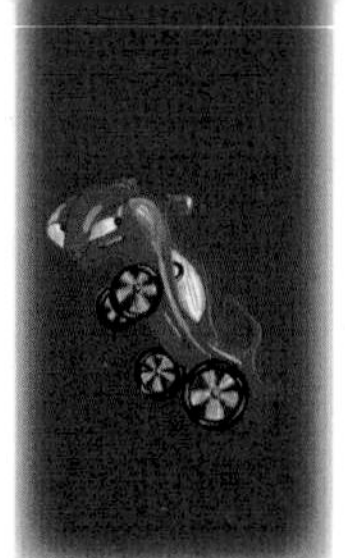

ROUND 6
CARS, PLANES, BOATS & TRAINS 15

QUESTIONS

1. British Airways used to be known as what?
2. In 1836, London's first public railway opened, what was it called?
3. What year was British Airways founded?
4. What year did Boeing launch the 747?
5. What percentage of total value of the world's manufactured exports is air freighted?
6. What year was the first in-flight meal served?
7. Which airport is Germany's biggest single-site employer?
8. The Concorde route between New York and London took how long?
9. Which high profile car company boss was arrested in 1982 on charges of drug trafficking?
10. What is the name of the French SNCF high speed train?

ANSWERS

1. British Overseas Airways Corporation (BOAC)
2. The London & Greenwich Railway.
3. 1952
4. 1969
5. 25%
6. 1935
7. Frankfurt
8. Three and a half hours
9. John De Lorean
10. TGV

ROUND 6
CARS, PLANES, BOATS & TRAINS 16

QUESTIONS

1. Which manufacturer was the first to use ABS brakes?
2. Which American car manufacturer opened a factory in Britain in 1911?
3. In the1960s, which designer epitomized the body styling skills of Ferrari?
4. What was the Spitfire's top speed?
5. What year did Ford first produce the Model T?
6. Where was Rolls Royce's first Silver Ghost built?
7. How many vehicles an hour does the M1 handle?
8. Volkswagen's name literally translated means what?
9. What car did 1970s TV cops Starsky and Hutch drive?
10. In which Bond movie was the famous Aston Martin introduced?

ANSWERS

1. Mercedes Benz
2. Ford
3. Battista "Pinin" Farina
4. 362mph at 29,000ft
5. 1908
6. Derby
7. 80,000
8. 'people's car'
9. Ford Torino
10. Goldfinger

ULTIMATE BRAINBUSTER

ROUND 7
ARTS & CRAFTS

ROUND 7
ARTS & CRAFTS 1

QUESTIONS

1. What year did Marcel Duchamp became a naturalized citizen of the United States?
2. What year was instant Poloroid photography introduced?
3. Who shot Andy Warhol on June 3, 1968?
4. Which artwork has the highest insurance value?
5. When was David Hockney born?
6. Who's work was stolen from the dining room at Rikers Island jail, by 4 prison guards?
7. After his death how much was Andy Warhol's estate auctioned for?
8. Which 20th century modernist sculptor is famous for his stick like figures?
9. Who screenprinted Elvis, Marilyn, Elizabeth Taylor and the Mona Lisa to name a few?
10. Which photographer wrote the trilogy of technical instruction manuals (The Camera, The Negative and The Print?

ANSWERS

1. 1955
2. 1947
3. Valerie Solanas
4. The Mona Lisa was insured for the value of $100 million
5. July 9, 1937
6. Salvador Dali's
7. Over 20 million dollars
8. Alberto Giacometti
9. Andy Warhol
10. Ansel Adams

ROUND 7
ARTS & CRAFTS 2

QUESTIONS

1. Which artist created the fashion magazine Interview?
2. What was the name of Dali's wife and muse?
3. Her Late Royal Highness The Princess Margaret was married to which aristocratic photographer?
4. Which eccentric pop artist is attributed with saying "I never think that people die. They just go to department stores"?
5. Bridget Riley is associated with which art movement?
6. Which photographer studied the movements of animals and humans using a series of cameras?
7. What year was sculptor Henry Moore born?
8. Where was Rossetti born?
9. Which American architect designed The Guaranty Building, Buffalo in 1894?
10. Where does the Mona Lisa hang?

ANSWERS

1. Andy Warhol
2. Gala
3. Lord Snowdon
4. Andy Warhol
5. Op Art
6. Eadweard Muybridge
7. 1898
8. London, England
9. Louis Henry Sullivan
10. Musée du Louvre in Paris

ROUND 7
ARTS & CRAFTS 3

QUESTIONS

1. What is the oil most commonly used in oil painting?
2. Which 60's British photographer directed the music video to Robert Palmer's "Addicted to Love"?
3. What is gouache?
4. What does the painting technique 'distemper' involve?
5. Who was the only person to buy a Van Gogh while he was alive?
6. What is a fresco painted on?
7. What does impasto mean in painting terms?
8. Which painter is the grandson of Sigmund Freud?
9. Which century was the Italian female painter Artemisia Gentileschi working?
10. What is the title of the only painting Van Gogh sold in his lifetime?

ANSWERS

1. Linseed
2. Terence Donovan
3. A type of opaque watercolour
4. The use of powdered colours mixed with glue size or egg yolk
5. His brother, Theo
6. Plaster
7. The paint is laid on thickly so texture stands out in relief
8. Lucien Freud
9. Seventeenth
10. "Red Vineyard at Arles"

ROUND 7
ARTS & CRAFTS 4

QUESTIONS

1. Which American photographer was a successful fashion model and fashion photographer who became a war photographer in World War II?
2. Who's painting 'Impression, Sunrise' of 1872 gave the Impressionist movement its name?
3. What is the name of the technique which uses minute points of pure colour that the eye then mixes for itself?
4. Who painted 'The Fighting Temeraire', 1839?
5. Which American photographer photographed herself in the bath in Adolf Hitler's former apartment in 1945?
6. Who designed Regent Street?
7. Who designed the Natural History Museum in London in 1868?
8. Which 20th century artist is associated with The Factory?
9. Which American photographer is famed for his stunning black & white landscape photographs of the national parks?
10. Who painted 'Water Lilly Pond' in 1889?

ANSWERS

1. Lee Miller
2. Claude Monet
3. Pointillism
4. J.M.W Turner
5. Lee Miller
6. John Nash
7. Alfred Waterhouse
8. Andy Warhol
9. Ansel Adams
10. Claude Monet

ROUND 7
ARTS & CRAFTS 5

QUESTIONS

1. Who designed the Guggenheim Museum in 1959?
2. Who designed 'La Sagrada Familia' in Barcelona?
3. Who made the world's first photograph in 1826?
4. In 1975 which British architect designed The Willis Faber Office, Ipswich?
5. What kind of photographic prints are egg whites used in?
6. Which British architect designed The Pompidou Centre in Paris in 1977?
7. 'Moonrise over Hernandez, New Mexico', 1941 is by which photographer?
8. What was stolen on August 22,1911 from the Musee du Louvre, Paris?
9. Which Hollywood actress did Cecil Beaton have a long affair with?
10. Which 'Young British Artist' made a sculpture of his own head made of frozen blood?

ANSWERS

1. Frank Lloyd Wright
2. Antonio Gaudi
3. Nicephore Niepce
4. Norman Foster
5. Albumen prints
6. Richard Rogers
7. Ansel Adams
8. The Mona Lisa
9. Greta Garbo
10. Mark Quinn

ROUND 7
ARTS & CRAFTS 6

QUESTIONS

1. Canaletto is famous for his paintings of which Italian city?
2. When the Mona Lisa was stolen in 1912, how many years was it before it was recovered?
3. Which 19th century English landscape painters' obsession with light turned his later work into almost abstract visions?
4. Which 'Young British Artist' famously exhibited her unmade bed at the Tate Gallery?
5. Which British fashion photographer said "The camera can be the most deadly weapon since the assassin's bullet. Or it can be the lotion of the heart"?
6. Which artist signed his 'Fountain' sculpture "R. Mutt"?
7. What city was the sculptor Rodin born in?
8. In 1956, what happened to the Mona Lisa?
9. Who painted 'The Grand Canal and the Church of the Salute', in 1730?
10. Who painted 'Les Desmoiselles d'Avignon' in 1907?

ANSWERS

1. Venice
2. Three
3. J.M.W Turner
4. Tracy Emin
5. Norman Parkinson
6. Marcel Duchamp
7. Paris
8. It was severely damaged after an acid attack
9. Canaletto
10. Pablo Picasso

ROUND 7
ARTS & CRAFTS 7

QUESTIONS

1. Who stole the Mona Lisa in 1911, by simply walking out the Louvre with it under his coat?
2. Who painted The Night Watch' in 1642?
3. How long did the Mona Lisa take to complete?
4. Which Eighteenth century Spanish painter painted almost the same painting twice, The Clothed Maja and The Nude Maja?
5. In 1938, Salvador Dali and Edward James designed a sofa based on who's lips?
6. Which dynamic abstract expressionist artist was also known as a gesture painter?
7. Which 18th century English painter specialized in horse paintings?
8. Who painted the series 'The Rakes Progress'?
9. Who said "In the future everyone will be world-famous for 15 minutes"?
10. The Vitruvian Man is a famous drawing by which artist?

ANSWERS

1. Louvre employee. Vincenzo Perugia
2. Rembrandt
3. Three or four years
4. Goya
5. Mae West
6. Jackson Pollock
7. George Stubbs
8. William Hogarth
9. Andy Warhol
10. Leonardo da Vinci

ROUND 7
ARTS & CRAFTS 8

QUESTIONS

1. Who designed the Glasgow School of Art in 1896?
2. Duane Hanson's sculptures are uncannily what?
3. Which pop artist is famed for his comic strip inspired paintings?
4. Who designed London's St Paul's Cathedral?
5. Which British photographer made the television commercial for the lynx anti-fur campaign - "It takes a dozen dumb animals to make a fur coat and just one to wear it"?
6. What year was Van Gogh born?
7. Frida Kahlo was a painter from which country?
8. Which political muralist painter was Frida Kahlo married to?
9. In 1982 who was given the title Marquis of Pubol?
10. What colour is vermillion?

ANSWERS

1. Charles Rennie Macintosh
2. Lifelike. Hanson belongs to the super-realist movement
3. Roy Lichenstein
4. Sir Christopher Wren
5. David Bailey
6. 1853
7. Mexico
8. Diego Rivera
9. Salvador Dali
10. Red

ROUND 7
ARTS & CRAFTS 9

QUESTIONS

1. What year was the Magnum photographic agency founded?
2. Who invented Poloroid instant process film?
3. Which pop artist was famous for his blonde wigs?
4. Who painted 'Dream Caused by the Flight of a Bumblebee around a Pomegranate a Second Before Awakening' in 1944?
5. Marcel Duchamp is known for his association with which artist group?
6. Which famous painter was left-handed and used mirror writing throughout his life?
7. Marcel Duchamp's work "In advance of a broken arm" was made from what?
8. Which artist had a 'blue period'?
9. Which post-impressionist painter has been called 'The Soul of Montmartre'?
10. Which painter produced all of his work (some 900 paintings and 1100 drawings) during a mere 10 years, then committed suicide?

ANSWERS

1. 1947
2. Dr Edwin Land
3. Andy Warhol
4. Salvador Dali
5. The Dadaists
6. Leonardo da Vinci
7. An old snow shovel
8. Picasso
9. Toulouse Lautrec
10. Vincent Van Gogh

ROUND 7
ARTS & CRAFTS 10

QUESTIONS

1. Which female photographer is famous for her photographs of Marilyn Monroe?
2. Who designed the Art Deco Midland Hotel in Morecambe, England?
3. What is the largest statue in the world?
4. On May 15, 1990 who's painting 'Portrait of Doctor Gachet' was sold for $82.5 at Christies?
5. Who designed Marble Arch?
6. Who said "You can't be more horrific than life itself."?
7. Which 1960's cockney photographer was part of 'swinging London'?
8. Who designed the Neo-Gothic Houses of Parliament at Westminster?
9. In the 1840's and 50's who led the Pre-Raphaelite movement?
10. Which shocking 20th century abstract painter is famous for his series painting of Popes and series in tryptichs?

ANSWERS

1. Eve Arnold
2. Oliver Hill
3. Mount Rushmore
4. Vincent Van Gogh
5. John Nash
6. Francis Bacon
7. David Bailey
8. Sir Charles Barry
9. Gabriel Rossetti
10. Francis Bacon

ROUND 7
ARTS & CRAFTS 11

QUESTIONS

1. Who carved the monumental statue of 'David' in Florence?
2. Which 18th century English satirist wrote The Analysis of Beauty, 1753?
3. Who painted the fresco ceiling of the Sistine Chapel?
4. What year was Carravaggio born?
5. Who designed the Chupa Chups logo in 1969?
6. Tempera is made from what?
7. What type of camera does Richard Avedon use for his portraits?
8. In 1623 which Spanish painter was court painter to King Phillip IV?
9. What was Rembrandt's full name?
10. What is the name for an element in art, defined as a very high contrast between light and dark?

ANSWERS

1. Michelangelo
2. William Hogarth
3. Michelangelo
4. 1573
5. Salvador Dali
6. Egg yolk
7. A large-format 8x10 view camera
8. Velazquez
9. Rembrandt Harmenszoon van Rijn
10. Chiaroscuro

ROUND 7
ARTS & CRAFTS 12

QUESTIONS

1. Who published the first photographic book in 1844, The Pencil of Nature?
2. Which 'Young British Artist' made a tent with the names of everyone she'd ever slept with stitched on it?
3. Which gallery is the Turner Prize held at?
4. Which cockney photographer published a book of pictures of his wife titled 'Trouble and Strife'?
5. Which 60's photographer took their own life, in November 22, 1996?
6. Which artist has had the most auction sales ever?
7. What is the most stolen artwork, having disappeared 4 times?
8. What painting sold at auction for $93 million, (£56 million)?
9. The most valuable pen and ink drawing sold at auction was Michaelangelo's 'Study of a mourning woman' 1494-1504. How much did it sell for in 2001?
10. Who had the largest simultaneous photo art exhibition with the same show on at 41 galleries around the world simultaneously in 1999?

ANSWERS

1. William Henry Fox Talbot
2. Tracey Emin
3. The Tate Gallery, London
4. David Bailey
5. Terence Donovan
6. Pablo Picasso
7. 'Jacob III de Cheyn' by Rembrandt
8. Picasso's 'Garcon a la Pipe' 1905
9. £5,943,500
10. Martin Parr's show 'Common Sense'

ROUND 7
ARTS & CRAFTS 13

QUESTIONS

1. How many paintings did John Constable sell in his lifetime?
2. Who was dubbed "Jack the Dripper" due to his painting style?
3. Which British architect designed the Lloyds building in London in 1986?
4. Who photographed Elizabeth II's Coronation in 1953?
5. Which artist together with Pablo Picasso developed Cubism?
6. Which painter died in an alcohol-related car crash in 1956?
7. Where was David Hockney born?
8. How old was Van Gogh when he shot himself?
9. Which British painter made a series of oil paintings of swimming pools in Los Angeles?
10. Which art school did Francis Bacon attend?

ANSWERS

1. Twenty
2. Jackson Pollock
3. Richard Rogers
4. Cecil Beaton
5. Georges Braque
6. Jackson Pollock
7. Bradford
8. 37
9. David Hockney
10. None, he was self taught

ROUND 7
ARTS & CRAFTS 14

QUESTIONS

1. What was Michelangelo's full name?
2. What year was the Mona Lisa completed?
3. Who said "Your first 10,000 photographs are your worst"?
4. In 1961 which painting hung upside-down for 2 months in the Museum of Modern Art, New York with none of the 116,000 visitors noticing?
5. Who painted 'The Potato Eaters', 1885?
6. Who made the first colour photograph in 1861?
7. What was the rebirth of classical art otherwise known as?
8. Where did the Renaissance begin?
9. What was the first object to be photographed in colour?
10. Which century did the Renaissance begin?

ANSWERS

1. Michelangelo di Lodovico Buonarroti Simoni
2. 1507
3. Henri Cartier-Bresson
4. Matisse's 'Le Bateau' (The Boat)
5. Vincent Van Gogh
6. James Maxwell
7. The Renaissance
8. Florence, Italy
9. A tartan ribbon
10. Fifteenth

ROUND 7
ARTS & CRAFTS 15

QUESTIONS

1. How old was Jackson Pollock when he died?
2. What is Turner's full name?
3. What makes up Marcel Duchamps work, 'Fountain'?
4. Which 19th century English landscape painter's dying words were reputedly "The Sun is God"?
5. Who designed Regents Park and it's terraces?
6. What was the name of Andy Warhol's famous studio?
7. In 1912, who painted 'Nude Descending a Staircase, No. 2'?
8. Who coined the phrase "The decisive moment" referring to taking photographs?
9. In 1965, which band did Andy Warhol manage?
10. Who painted 'The Hay Wain'?

ANSWERS

1. 44
2. Joseph Mallord William Turner
3. A ceramic urinal
4. J.M.W Turner
5. John Nash
6. The Factory
7. Marcel Duchamp
8. Henri Cartier-Bresson
9. The Velvet Underground
10. John Constable

ROUND 7
ARTS & CRAFTS 16

QUESTIONS

1. How did the prolific sculptor Rodin die?
2. What year did Picasso die?
3. Where was Van Gogh born?
4. Toulouse-Laurtrec is famous for painting the low life and dance halls of which city?
5. Which 18th horse painter studied anatomy and taught it at a hospital in York?
6. Which post impressionist painter is famous for his colourful works from the South Seas?
7. Which Parisian painter was only 4 1/2 feet (1.5 meters) tall?
8. Salvador Dali belonged to which group of artists?
9. What age was Picasso when he died?
10. Which influencial photographer and founding member of Magnum photographic agency died in 2004?

ANSWERS

1. Frostbite
2. 1973
3. Zundert in the Netherlands
4. Paris
5. George Stubbs
6. Paul Gaugin
7. Toulouse Lautrec
8. The Surrealists
9. 92
10. Henri Cartier-Bresson

ROUND 7
ARTS & CRAFTS 17

QUESTIONS

1. Which Leonardo da Vinci painting can be found in the refectory of the convent of Santa Maria delle Grazie in Milan?
2. Which 1936 painting by Picasso depicts the horrors of the Spanish Civil War?
3. Who did Jackson Pollock marry in 1944?
4. Who invented The Zone System?
5. In 1919, which famous Dadaist artist parodied the Mona Lisa with a moustache and a goatee?
6. Which 'Young British Artist' exhibited a shark in formaldehyde?
7. Which group of painters were also known as 'Wild Beasts'?
8. In December 2004, which art work was voted most influential of the 20th century?
9. Who painted a picture of a pipe titled 'Ceci n'est pas une pipe (The Betrayal Of Images)' (1928-1929)?
10. On March 30, 1987 Van Gogh's painting 'Irises' was sold for how much at Sothebys, New York?

ANSWERS

1. The Last Supper
2. Guernica
3. Lee Krasner
4. Ansel Adams
5. Marcel Duchamp
6. Damien Hirst
7. The Fauves
8. Marcel Duchamp's 'Fountain'
9. Rene Magritte
10. US$53.9 million

ROUND 7
ARTS & CRAFTS 18

QUESTIONS

1. Who painted 'The Birth of Venus' in 1482?
2. What year was the Mona Lisa painting started?
3. What painting is known a 'La Joconde' in French?
4. Who painted 'The Last Supper'?
5. Which painted subject is known for her "enigmatic smile"
6. Which English romantic landscape painter never married but had two daughters with his mistress Sarah Danby?
7. What year did Leonardo da Vinci begin painting 'The Last Supper'?
8. What is the largest hammered copper statue in the world?
9. What date was Vincent van Gogh born?
10. Which iconic artwork depicts a naked male figure in two superimposed positions with his arms apart and simultaneously inscribed in a circle and square?

ANSWERS

1. Botticelli
2. 1503
3. Mona Lisa
4. Leonardo da Vinci
5. The Mona Lisa
6. J.M.W Turner
7. 1495
8. The Statue of Liberty
9. March 30, 1853
10. The Vitruvian Man by Leonardo da Vinci

ROUND 8

SCIENCE & NATURE

$E = Mc^2$

ROUND 8
SCIENCE & NATURE 1

QUESTIONS

1. Which four planets are closest to the Sun?
2. What is the largest species of bird in the world?
3. Which garden vegetable aided Gregor Mendel is his discovery of some simple rules by which genes are inherited?
4. What is the name of the hormone secreted by the ovaries?
5. What is the standard equation used to calculate speed?
6. What is the boiling point of water, at standard pressure, in degrees Fahrenheit?
7. Which gas is used to fill most domestic light bulbs?
8. What are the four letters of the DNA alphabet, used to write the genetic code?
9. What is the atomic number of the element carbon?
10. Which type of light has a longer wavelength, ultra violet or infrared?

ANSWERS

1. Mercury, Venus, Earth and Mars
2. The ostrich
3. The pea
4. Oestrogen
5. Speed = distance/time (Speed = Distance divided by time)
6. 212°F
7. Argon
8. G,A,T and C
9. 6
10. Infrared

ROUND 8
SCIENCE & NATURE 2

QUESTIONS

1. What hormone controls puberty in males?
2. Which organ of the body has the following functions - to get rid of toxins, to regulate your blood sugar levels and to produce bile?
3. On 30th December 1995, Altnaharra in the Scottish Highlands experienced a record low UK temperature. What was it?
4. What is the name given to the cells in planets whose specific function is to carry out photosynthesis?
5. What was the first SSRI anti-depressant?
6. What is the collective name given to soft-bodied invertebrates, many of which live in calcareous shells?
7. What are the four main food types?
8. In which part of the body is the humerus?
9. By how many degrees does the Intergovernmental Panel on Climate Change predict that global temperature will rise by the end of this century?
10. In the human body, what are proteins required for?

1. Testosterone
2. The liver
3. -27.2 °C
4. Palisade cells
5. Prozac (Fluoxetine)
6. Molluscs
7. Carbohydrates, fats, proteins and fibres
8. The arm
9. Between 1.4°C and 5.8°C

Growth and repair

ROUND 8
SCIENCE & NATURE 3

QUESTIONS

1. What type of high frequency waves can be used as medical tracers, to kill cancer cells or to image defects in metal?
2. Which cells in the human body contain haemoglobin?
3. Which gland in the brain is stimulated by sunlight?
4. Lithium, sodium, potassium, rubidium, caesium and francium are collectively known as what type of metals?
5. What do the initials AC and DC stand for?
6. What are phloem vessels?
7. What causes a suntan?
8. Sunlight is our main source of which vitamin?
9. Who established the first mathematical formulation of the theory of gravitation?
10. What is the boiling point, measured at normal pressure, of mercury?

ANSWERS

1. Gamma rays
2. Red blood cells
3. The pineal gland
4. Alkali metals
5. Alternating current and Direct current
6. They are the vein-like structures through which food is distributed
7. Ultra violet light stimulating the body's melanin production
8. Vitamin D
9. Isaac Newton
10. 357°C

ROUND 8
SCIENCE & NATURE 4

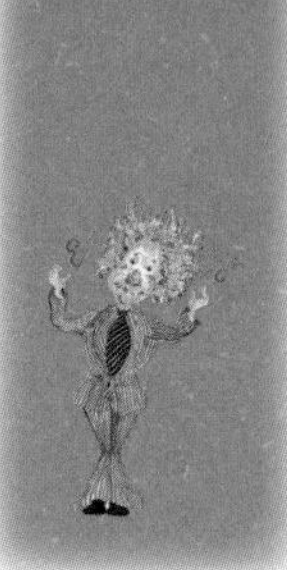

QUESTIONS

1. How long is there between high tides?
2. By 2010 3% of the UK's electricity will come from what source?
3. What is the unit of measurement used to express the frequency of light waves?
4. What is the Latin (or Genus) name for the poppy?
5. Which planet in the Solar System isn't named after a god?
6. At standard temperature and pressure is Bromine a solid, liquid or gas?
7. How was Dutch Elm Disease spread?
8. In which country is the magnetic north pole?
9. Where did David Scott famously repeat Galileo's supposed experiment to establish a theory of gravity by dropping a feather and a hammer from each hand at the same time?
10. What is the name given to the cells in the human body whose purpose is to fight disease, either by engulfing bacteria or making antibodies?

ANSWERS

1. 12 hours 25 minutes
2. Wind power
3. Hertz (Hz)
4. Papaver
5. Earth
6. Liquid
7. By bark beetles
8. Canada
9. On the surface of the moon
10. White blood cells

ROUND 8
SCIENCE & NATURE 5

QUESTIONS

1. In which part of the body are the fibula and tibia bones?
2. What bone is the patella?
3. How is the unit of measurement of acceleration normally expressed?
4. A tree's age can be determined by counting its 'rings' – what causes these 'rings' to form?
5. Every square centimetre of skin contains 15 receptors for pressure, 6 receptors for cold and how many receptors for warmth?
6. In which year did Louis Pasteur and Claude Bernard complete their first test on pasteurisation?
7. Energy from the sun travels towards Earth via ultra violet radiation – what are the three types of ultra violet radiation?
8. Which organ accounts for around 16% of a persons body weight?
9. In the periodic table what does the symbol Fe stand for?
10. The heart is divided into four chambers, the upper two are called atria. What are the lower two chambers called?

ANSWERS

1. The legs
2. The kneecap
3. Metres per second per second or m/s_
4. The slowing of the tree's growth in winter, and the speeding up of its growth in spring
5. One
6. 1862
7. UV-A, UV-B and UV-C
8. The skin
9. Iron
10. Ventricles

ROUND 8
SCIENCE & NATURE 6

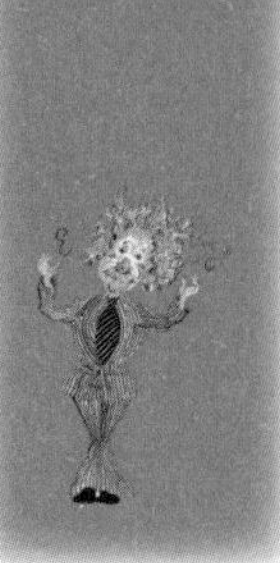

QUESTIONS

1. In which part of the body can the Epiglotis be found?
2. What is mass the measurement of?
3. What is the most common blood type group in the UK?
4. In the desert, what meteorological phenomenon occurs when air near the ground is hotter than air higher up?
5. What is the name given to the thin line of cloud that forms behind an aircraft at high altitudes?
6. Which ocean current influences the climate of the UK and northwest Europe by bringing with it humid mild air?
7. What is the name given to the largest part of the human brain?
8. During a total solar eclipse, by how many degrees can the temperature drop?
9. How many feet are in 3 fathoms?
10. What is the function of the region of the brain known as the occipital lobe?

ANSWERS

1. The throat
2. How much matter a body has
3. O+ (37% of the population)
4. A mirage
5. A contrail
6. The Gulf Stream
7. The cerebrum
8. 6°C or 20°F
9. 18 (1 fathom = 6 feet)
10. The detection and interpretation of visual images

ROUND 8
SCIENCE & NATURE 7

QUESTIONS

1. By what name is the tuberculosis vaccine known?
2. Which three illnesses does the MMR vaccine protect against?
3. Do we inherit our mitochondrial DNA only from our mothers or our fathers?
4. What is the largest bone in the human body?
5. Which German physicist discovered ultra violet radiation?
6. Why are fungi not classified as plants?
7. Helium, neon, argon, krypton, xenon and radon are collectively known as what type of gases?
8. What is the name given to the rare autoimmune disorder that causes small blood vessels around the body to become inflamed?
9. What is the name given to the land under the ocean at the edge of the continental masses?
10. What is the name given to the condition in which disturbances in the brain's normal electrical activity lead to recurrent fits or brief episodes of altered consciousness?

ANSWERS

1. The BCG vaccine
2. Measles, mumps and rubella
3. Mothers
4. The femur (or thighbone)
5. Johann Ritter
6. Because they do not contain the green pigment called chlorophyll
7. Noble gases
8. Behcet's disease
9. Continental shelf
10. Epilepsy

ROUND 8
SCIENCE & NATURE 8

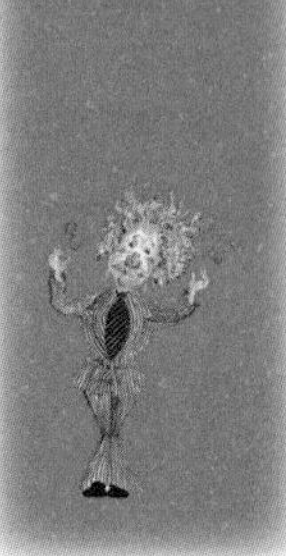

QUESTIONS

1. Of the 6000 spawn laid by a frog, around how many of these will become adult frogs?
2. What accidental discovery led Crawford Long to develop surgical anaesthesia in 1842?
3. What form of energy is stored in an object when it is lifted, stretched or squashed?
4. What is the Latin (or Genus) name for the daffodil?
5. Which nerve transmits nerve impulses from the eye to the brain?
6. How many bones make up the human skeleton?
7. What is the name of the green chemical that enables photosynthesis to take place in plants?
8. What is the specific function of a nerve cell?
9. What are a fishes pectoral fins used for?
10. Are fish poikilothermic or homeothermic creatures?

ANSWERS

1. 6
2. He hurt himself, but felt no pain while under the influence of ether at a party
3. Potential energy
4. Narcissus
5. The optic nerve
6. 206
7. Chlorophyll
8. To pass sensory impulses from receptor to effector
9. Steering and balance
10. Poikilothermic (cold blooded)

ROUND 8
SCIENCE & NATURE 9

QUESTIONS

1. What are the five primary tastes that our tastebuds detect?
2. Lateral Epicondylitis is the medical name for which common medical condition?
3. Why is the left lung smaller than the right lung?
4. What are the names of the three processes used to describe different types of thermal energy transfer?
5. In 1753, which Swedish naturalist published the system of plant naming and classification still in use today?
6. What is the main function of the bladder?
7. What is the name given to the proteins which catalyse or speed up chemical reactions inside our bodies?
8. Who was the first woman to hold the post of Professor of General Physics in the Faculty of Sciences at the Sorbonne in Paris?
9. Which type of eagle has a crest of white feathers on its head?
10. What might be called Dihydrogen Monoxide?

ANSWERS

1. Sour, sweet, bitter, salty and umami
2. Tennis elbow
3. To make space for the heart
4. Conduction, convection and radiation
5. Carl Linnaeus
6. For storing urine
7. Enzymes
8. Marie Curie
9. The bald eagle
10. Water

ROUND 8
SCIENCE & NATURE 10

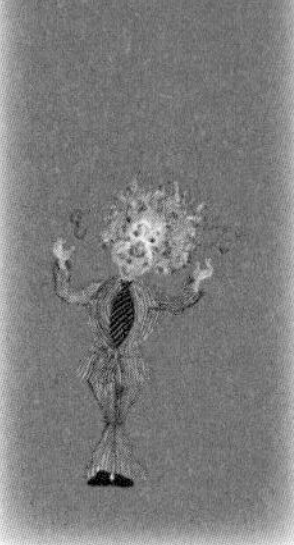

QUESTIONS

1. In 1983, which company announced that they had created the first genetically modified plant?
2. Name the three crew members of the lunar landing.
3. Ultra violet radiation from the sun is strongest between which hours of the day?
4. In which year will Halley's comet next be visible from Earth?
5. British scientist developed DNA profiling, in 1984?
6. Forests dating from before 1700AD are defined as what type of woodland?
7. What is the name of the 17mile high extinct volcano on Mars?
8. What is the montane zone?
9. In the periodic table what does the symbol Cu stand for?
10. Which letters represent the metal gold in the periodic table?

ANSWERS

1. Monsanto
2. Neil Armstrong, Buzz Aldrin and Michael Collins
3. 10am to 4pm
4. 2061
5. Alec Jeffries
6. Ancient woodland
7. Olympus Mons
8. Land 600m above sea level
9. Copper
10. Au

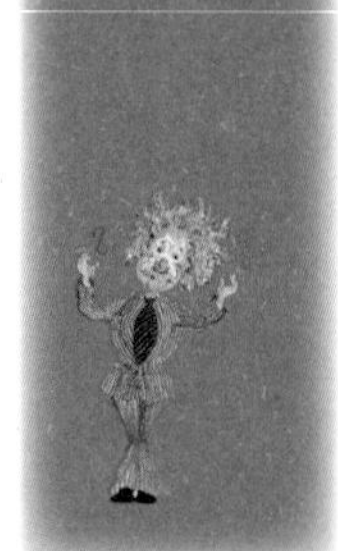

ROUND 8
SCIENCE & NATURE 11

QUESTIONS

1. What are the two types of fibre in human muscle?
2. What are the skeletons of skates and rays made from?
3. What are the two broad categories of plants?
4. A tornado with wind speeds of between 261mph and 318mph is classed as what type of tornado?
5. In the periodic table what does the symbol K stand for?
6. What is another name for the voice box?
7. Name two artificial/man made objects visible on the Earth's surface from space?
8. What meteorological phenomenon is the 'Great Red Spot' on the surface of Jupiter?
9. Which is the only planet that spins in the same direction as it travels?
10. What is the name given to lowest temperature at which substances contain no heat energy?

ANSWERS

1. Slow twitch muscle fibre and fast twitch muscle fibre
2. Cartilage
3. Flowering and non-flowering
4. An F5 Tornado
5. Potassium
6. The larynx
7. The Great Wall of China and the Egyptian pyramids
8. A thunderstorm
9. Uranus
10. Absolute zero

ROUND 8
SCIENCE & NATURE 12

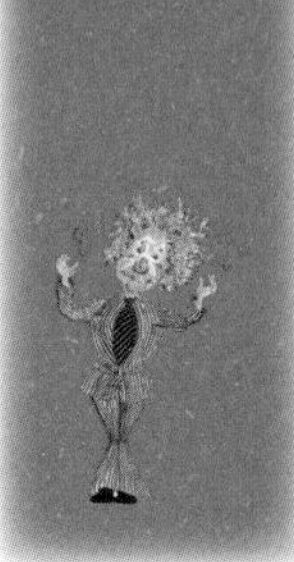

QUESTIONS

1. What is the name of the part of the inner ear where the actual organ of hearing is located?
2. Which virus family causes cold sores?
3. Which great historical work of art includes a depiction of a sighting of Halley's comet?
4. In which year was the Nobel Prize in Medicine won by Richard Axel and Linda B Buck, for their work on smell?
5. What is the name of the respiratory organ found in many aquatic animals?
6. What does the chemical oestrogen process in your body?
7. Thyroxine is secreted by which gland in the human body?
8. In which part of the body can the deltoid muscles be found?
9. What percentage of the human DNA sequence is shared with that of chimpanzees?
10. Which medical condition occurs when the pancreas doesn't make enough, or any, of the hormone insulin?

ANSWERS

1. Cochlea
2. Herpes
3. The Bayeux tapestry
4. 2004
5. Gills
6. Hormones
7. The thyroid gland
8. The shoulders
9. 98%
10. Diabetes

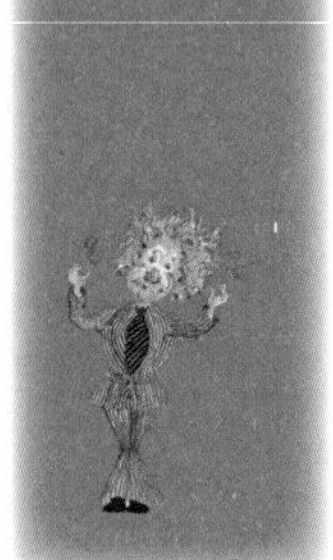

ROUND 8
SCIENCE & NATURE 13

QUESTIONS

1. What are sea mounts?
2. Aside from the risk of developing skin cancer, what other medical condition has been linked to high levels of exposure to the sun?
3. In 1895, who discovered X-rays?
4. Throughout the tropical world, what disease is the most common infective killer?
5. What is considered a normal resting heart rate for women?
6. Algin, a starch-like chemical contained in kelp, can be used as a thickening agent in which food?
7. What are the names of the two regions of the Solar System from which comets originate?
8. Which planet in the Solar System has the most moons?
9. What is the first element of the standard periodic table?
10. When included in the naming of a plant, what does the Latin epithet quadrifolius describe?

ANSWERS

1. Underwater volcanoes
2. Cataracts
3. Wilhelm Röntgen
4. Malaria
5. 72-80 beats per minute
6. Ice-cream
7. The Kuiper Belt and the Oort cloud
8. Jupiter
9. Hydrogen
10. Four leaves (a plant with leaves in formations of four)

ROUND 8
SCIENCE & NATURE 14

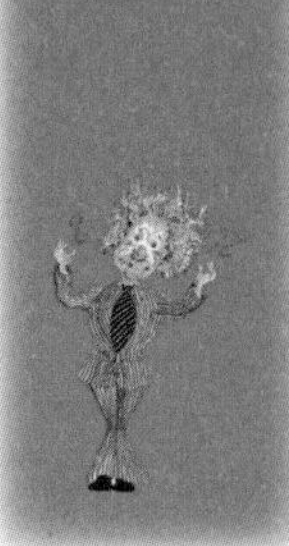

QUESTIONS

1. It is the presence or absence of which chromosome, the X or Y, that determines a person's sex?
2. What is the largest animal ever to live on Earth?
3. What is the name of the formula, used to describe the relationship between voltage, current and resistance, written R = V/I or I = V/R?
4. In Ecological terms, what is the definition of the word habitat?
5. What is the name given to the nest of a bird, such as an eagle, built on a cliff or other high place?
6. What type of tree is the tallest tree in the world?
7. Which chemical element is Albertus Magnus believed to have been the first to isolate in 1250?
8. Who discovered oxygen, in 1771?
9. What colour are the buds of an Ash tree?
10. How many receptors for pain are contained within the same square centimetre of skin?

ANSWERS

1. Y
2. The blue whale
3. Ohm's Law
4. It means a place where plants and animals live
5. An eyrie
6. The Coast Redwood
7. Arsenic
8. Joseph Priestly
9. Black
10. 200

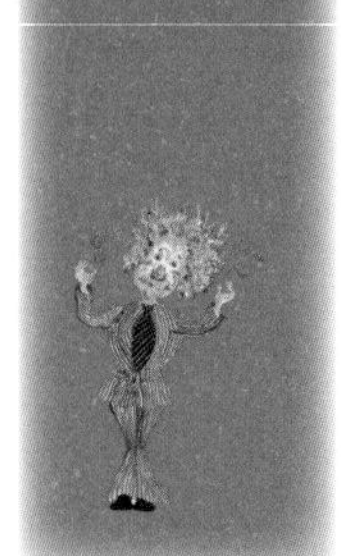

ROUND 8
SCIENCE & NATURE 15

QUESTIONS

1. What is the pH value of pure water?
2. Which organs of the body makes urine from waste products and the excess water found in your blood?
3. What is the chemical symbol of sodium chloride (ordinary table salt)?
4. What is the reported maximum age of Haddock?
5. Where in the UK was the highest temperature of 38.5°C recorded, on 10th August 2003?
6. Is the vast majority of ozone in the Earth's atmosphere contained within the troposphere or the stratosphere?
7. Which Greek philosophers view of the universe did Galileo set out to disprove by experiment?
8. What was discovered, in 1824, by Jean-Baptiste Joseph Fourier?
9. What form of energy is output from a cooker?
10. What colour of flower does the Latin epithet aureus describe?

ANSWERS

1. 7
2. The kidneys
3. $NaCl$
4. 20 years
5. Brogdale, near Faversham in Kent
6. The stratosphere (90% of ozone is contained here)
7. Aristotle
8. The greenhouse effect
9. Heat
10. Golden yellow

ROUND 8
SCIENCE & NATURE 16

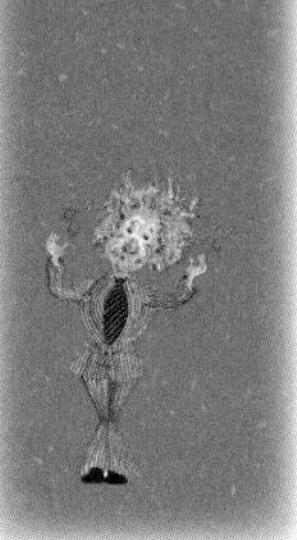

QUESTIONS

1. In which British seaside resort was the highest monthly total of hours of sunshine recorded in 1911?
2. What was the one of the main factors that contributed to the widespread use of safe penicillin, developed in Britain and the US during WW2?
3. What is the approximate speed of light?
4. Sea kale is a member of which plant family?
5. What forms the basis of a walrus' diet?
6. According to legend, which historic monument is said to have played a part in the development of Galileo's theory of gravity?
7. The 'asteroid belt', containing 90-95% of all asteroids in our Solar System, is found between which two planets?
8. Why did the early Christian church ban the use of mistletoe?
9. How did Alexander Fleming start making his discovery of penicillin?
10. What word describes farmland planted with crops?

ANSWERS

1. Eastbourne
2. It was not patented, and could therefore be made cheaply
3. 300,000km per second / 186,300 miles per second
4. Cabbage
5. Sand mussels
6. The Tower of Pisa
7. Mars and Jupiter
8. Because of its association with Druids.
9. From the observation that mould growing in petri dishes stacked in his laboratory sink had killed the staph bacteria previously contained in these petri dishes
10. Arable land

ROUND 8
SCIENCE & NATURE 17

QUESTIONS

1. Which species of bird has the longest wingspan?
2. Who developed the smallpox vaccine?
3. What part of the Earth's atmosphere was discovered in 1913 by two French physicists, Charles Fabry and Henri Buisson?
4. What does the nucleus of an atom consist of?
5. Although they can not fly, what is the top speed that ostriches have been measured running at?
6. Who, and what, was the first mammal to be cloned from an adult cell?
7. What disease did Jonas E Salk discover the cure for in 1952?
8. How long do simple fractures usually take to heal?
9. What are the names of Mars' two moons?
10. Which has the lower pH value – limejuice or milk of magnesium?

ANSWERS

1. The albatross
2. Edward Jenner
3. The ozone layer
4. Protons and neutrons
5. 45mph
6. Dolly the sheep
7. Polio
8. About 6-8 weeks
9. Deimos and Phobos
10. Limejuice

ROUND 8
SCIENCE & NATURE 18

QUESTIONS

1. In which year was the Hubble telescope launched?
2. What do the initials N.A.S.A. stand for?
3. Which gas forms 78% of the Earth's atmosphere?
4. In which English county can The Fens be found?
5. Where in the world are the two great continental ice sheets situated?
6. Which organ of the body has the following function - to store and concentrate bile produced in your liver?
7. What is the name of the scale used to measure the intensity of a tornado?
8. Which letter or letters represent the gas Nitrogen in the periodic table?
9. Which Apollo mission was the first manned lunar landing?
10. What meteorological phenomenon occurs when warm and cool airstreams collide to create a rotating area of low atmospheric pressure?

ANSWERS

1. 1990
2. National Aeronautics and Space Administration
3. Nitrogen
4. East Anglia
5. The Antarctic and Greenland
6. The gall bladder
7. The Fujita Scale
8. N
9. Apollo 11
10. Tornadoes

ULTIMATE
BRAINBUSTER

ROUND 9
SOCCER

ROUND 9
SOCCER 1

QUESTIONS

1. What year was Wayne Rooney born?
2. From which Italian football team did Sven Goran Eriksson resign as manager in 2001?
3. Which city hosted the 2001 Cup Final?
4. Which British football team won the European Cup in 1967?
5. Which football teams home ground is Prenton Park?
6. In May 1998, against which country was Michael Owen's goal that made him the youngest player to score for England?
7. Which club bought Kevin Campbell from Arsenal?
8. Which French footballer scored twice in the 1998 World Cup final?
9. Which football club beat Birmingham City on penalties to win the 2001 Worthington Cup?
10. Which team did England beat in Sven Goran Eriksson's first game as coach?

ANSWERS

1. 1985
2. Lazio
3. Cardiff
4. Celtic
5. Tranmere Rovers
6. Morocco
7. Nottingham Forest
8. Zinedine Zidane
9. Liverpool
10. Spain

ROUND 9
SOCCER 2

QUESTIONS

1. Who is Stoke City's most capped player?
2. Who scored eight goals in a game for Celtic against Dunfermline in 1928?
3. Who scored the first ever goal in a Wembley FA Cup final?
4. How many caps did Bryan Robson win for England?
5. What year did Ireland first play England?
6. Who is Walsall's most capped player?
7. How many caps did Bobby Robson win for England?
8. Which English club is otherwise know as The Tigers?
9. Who is Dundee's most capped player?
10. In 1931, which Celtic goalkeeper died accidentally in a game against Rangers?

ANSWERS

1. Gordon Banks
2. Jimmy McGrory
3. David Jack
4. 90
5. 1882
6. Mick Kearns
7. 20
8. Hull City
9. Alex Hamilton
10. John Thomson

ROUND 9
SOCCER 3

QUESTIONS

1. From which club did Aston Villa sign Juan Pablo Angel?
2. In which year did Newcastle United sign Alan Shearer?
3. Which former Middlesborough and Newcastle player was controversially left out of the 1998 England World Cup squad?
4. Who won the FA Cup in 1969?
5. Which newly promoted team topped the English Premiership after the first Saturday of the 2000-2001 season?
6. Who captained Fulham in the 1975 FA Cup final?
7. Which Manchester United player was named Footballer of the year and PFA Footballer of the Year in 2000?
8. From which club did Kenny Dalglish join Liverpool in 1977?
9. Which Czech club did Josef Chovanec become coach of in 1996/7?
10. After which former player is Real Madrid's stadium named?

ANSWERS

1. River Plate
2. 1996
3. Paul Gasgoigne
4. Manchester City
5. Charlton Athletic
6. Bobby Moore
7. Roy Keane
8. Celtic
9. Sparta Prague
10. Santiago Bernabeu

ROUND 9
SOCCER 4

QUESTIONS

1. Who was the European Footballer of the Year in 1968?
2. What nationality is footballer Paolo Di Canio?
3. Which former manager of Wolverhampton Wanderers died in 2001 at the age of 85?
4. Who was the England football coach for one match between the reigns of Glenn Hoddle and Kevin Keegan?
5. Who won the FA Cup in 2000?
6. Which country won the 1970 world cup?
7. Which club signed Alan Kennedy from Newcastle United?
8. Who became Manager of Liverpool in 1959?
9. Which Spanish football club won the European Cup for the first time in 32 years in 1998?
10. What is the nickname of Bristol City football club?

ANSWERS

1. George Best
2. Italian
3. Stan Cullis
4. Howard Wilkinson
5. Chelsea
6. Brazil
7. Liverpool
8. Bill Shankley
9. Real Madrid
10. The Robins

ROUND 9
SOCCER 5

QUESTIONS

1. Which club bought David Batty from Newcastle United in 1998?
2. Which football club did Alf Garnett support?
3. Which Everton player scored the only goal in the 1995 FA Cup Final?
4. Who refereed the 2001 Worthington Cup final between Birmingham City and Liverpool?
5. Which team beat Tottenham Hotspur in the 2000/1 FA Cup semi finals?
6. Who replaced Terry Venables as England coach?
7. Which team did Johann Gruyff Captain the final of the 1974 World Cup?
8. Which football teams ground is call Roots Hall?
9. Which goalkeeper won 125 caps for England?
10. Who scored two penalties in the 1994 Cup Final?

ANSWERS

1. Leeds United
2. West Ham
3. Paul Rideout
4. David Elleray
5. Arsenal
6. Glen Hoddle
7. The Netherlands
8. Southend United's
9. Peter Shilton
10. Eric Cantona

ROUND 9
SOCCER 6

QUESTIONS

1. Who was the boss of Reading from 1963-69?
2. In 1994 which player was bought from Bradford City by Manchester United?
3. Which team did Tranmere beat 13-0 in the 1914 FA Cup?
4. Paul Scholes was born in which year?
5. Who is Oldham's most capped player?
6. Malcolm Allison was the boss at which club from 1992-93?
7. Who was boss at Blackburn Rovers from 1967-70?
8. In which year were Birmingham and Blackburn founded?
9. Who made 761 league appearances for Port Vale from 1950-72?
10. From which club did Crewe obtain David Platt on a free transfer?

ANSWERS

1. Roy Bentley
2. Graeme Tomlinson
3. Oswestry
4. 1974
5. Gunnar Halle
6. Bristol Rovers
7. Eddie Quigley
8. 1875
9. Roy Sproson
10. Manchester United

ROUND 9
SOCCER 7

QUESTIONS

1. Who is Liverpool's most capped player?
2. Who is Aberdeen's most capped player?
3. How many caps did Kenny Dalglish win for Scotland?
4. What year was Tom Finney born?
5. In which country was Danny Rodriguez born?
6. How many times did Stuart McCall score for Everton in the 1989 FA Cup final?
7. Which Preston goalkeeper wore glasses in the 1922 FA Cup Final against Huddersfield?
8. From 1930-1998, Brazil have played 80 games in World Cup final appearances. How many have they won?
9. How many goals were scored in the 1934 World Cup Finals?
10. Who scored for Nottingham Forest in the 1991 FA Cup Final against Nottingham?

ANSWERS

1. Ian Rush
2. Alex McLeish
3. 102
4. 1922
5. Portugal
6. Twice
7. J.F.Mitchell
8. 53
9. 70
10. Stuart Pearce

ROUND 9
SOCCER 8

QUESTIONS

1. In the six years from 1985-90, how many times were Bayern Munich crowned German League Champions?
2. Which club played at the De Meer stadium until 1996?
3. Which Irish side were known as 'Coad's Colts' in the 1950's?
4. Who took over from Raddy Antic as boss of Athletico Madrid?
5. In which year were Benfica founded?
6. Who became coach of AEK Athens in autumn 1998?
7. Which teams contested the 1998 Greek Cup Final?
8. In which country do Fortuna Sitard play?
9. Pyunik are a league club in which country?
10. In which year did Valencia first win the Spanish Cup?

ANSWERS

1. Five
2. Ajax
3. Shamrock Rovers
4. Arrigo Sacchi
5. 1904
6. Oleg Blokhin
7. Panionios and Panathinaikos
8. Netherlands
9. Armenia
10. 1941

ROUND 9
SOCCER 9

QUESTIONS

1. Who resigned as England football manager in 2000?
2. Adrian Boothroyd is the new Manager of which football club?
3. Which Liverpool player made 366 consecutive league appearances for the club from 1975 to 1983?
4. Which Dutch footballer was the European Footballer of the Year 1971,1973 and 1974?
5. Which former England football captain was a consultant on 'Valiant', an animated movie about World War II carrier pigeons?
6. Which team smashed their transfer record by signing Sergei Robrov from Dynamo Kiev?
7. Who scored Chelsea's winning goal in the 2000 FA Cup final?
8. Which Romanian footballer was sent off in the 2000 UEFA Cup final?
9. Which team knocked Newcastle United out of the Worthington Cup in two successive seasons?
10. Which country does footballer Paulo Wanchope represent?

ANSWERS

1. Kevin Keegan
2. Watford
3. Phil Neal
4. Johan Cruyff
5. Gerry Francis
6. Tottenham Hotspur
7. Roberto Di Matteo
8. Gheoghe Hagi
9. Birmingham City
10. Costa Rica

ROUND 9
SOCCER 10

QUESTIONS

1. Which club did Terry Venables manage to European success in 1986?
2. Which football team is nicknamed The Owls?
3. Who scored Scotland's only goal in Euro '96?
4. On the last day of the 1999/2000, Bradford City's Premiership survival was secured by victory against which team?
5. Which Welsh international footballer is nephew of former jockey John Francome?
6. For which club did Ashley Cole play on loan in 2000?
7. At which Premiership club is Gordon Milne Director of Football?
8. In February 2000, which former England footballer was sacked as coach by Celtic?
9. Which country beat Nigeria on penalties to win the 2000 African Nations Cup?
10. Which struggling football sacked Team Manager Egil Olsen in April 2000?

ANSWERS

1. Barcelona
2. Sheffield Wednesday
3. Ally McCoist
4. Liverpool
5. Sam Ricketts of Swansea City
6. Crystal Palace
7. Newcastle United
8. John Barnes
9. Cameroon
10. Wimbledon

ROUND 9
SOCCER 11

QUESTIONS

1. Which club did Swede Jonas Thern join in 1989?
2. With which club did Jackie Milburn spend his entire career?
3. How many goals were scored in the 1950 World Cup Finals?
4. Which non league club did Bruce Grbbelaar join in August 1998?
5. In 1974, Ron Atkinson took over as boss of which club?
6. Which player did Aston Villa buy from Sheffield Wednesday in 1994?
7. In which city was Alan Shearer born?
8. Who scored two penalties in the 1949 Scottish Cup final?
9. In which year was England centre forward Nat Lofthouse born?
10. Gordon Jago was boss at which club from 1974-77?

ANSWERS

1. Benfica
2. Newcastle United
3. 88
4. Chesham
5. Cambridge United
6. Ian Taylor
7. Southampton
8. George Young
9. 1925
10. Millwall

ROUND 9
SOCCER 12

QUESTIONS

1. In which year did Madrid FC adopt the prefix 'Real'?
2. Which team won The Italian League from 1931-35?
3. Which Hungarian team reached the semi-finals of the 1957/58 European Cup?
4. Silkeborg are a league club in which country?
5. In what colour striped shirts do Club Bruges of Belgium play?
6. In which city are Spanish club Real Betis based?
7. Which former England player missed a penalty for Torino in 1997/8 which kept the club in Serie B?
8. Which country did midfielder Antonin Panenka represent?
9. To which club did Matthias Sammer move in 1989?
10. Which Czech team merged with Pribram in 1997?

ANSWERS

1. 1920
2. Juventus
3. Vasas
4. Denmark
5. Blue and Black
6. Seville
7. Tony Dorigo
8. Czechoslovakia
9. Stuttgart
10. Dukla Prague

ROUND 9
SOCCER 13

QUESTIONS

1. Which football team was known as The Dons?
2. Which German football team knocked Manchester United out of the 2000/1 Champions League?
3. Which football team clinched the 2000/1 Premiership title with 5 games still to play?
4. Which Leicester goal keeper weighed over 52 stone when he died in 1809?
5. Which country did Mark Wright score the winning goal against in the 1990 World Cup?
6. Who did Joe Fagan succeed as manager of Liverpool football club?
7. What year was the FA Cup final first held?
8. From which club did Liverpool sign Stan Collymore for £8.5 million in 1995?
9. Who was Manager of the England football team from 1982 to 1990?
10. Who briefly played professional football at Scunthorpe United before becoming an International England Cricketer?

ANSWERS

1. Wimbledon (now MK Dons)
2. Bayern Munich
3. Manchester United
4. Daniel Lambert
5. Egypt
6. Bob Paisley
7. 1871
8. Nottingham Forest
9. Bobby Robson
10. Ian Botham

ROUND 9
SOCCER 14

QUESTIONS

1. Who is Southend United's most capped player?
2. Who is Manchester City's most capped player?
3. How many goals were scored in the 1962 World Cup Finals?
4. Who is Sheffield Wednesday's most capped player?
5. Which team beat Bristol Rovers 9-0 in October 1977?
6. Who is Manchester United's most capped player?
7. How many times did Bobby Moore play for the England youth team?
8. What year did Bruce Rioch take over at Bolton Wanderers?
9. Who is Norwich City's most capped player?
10. Which animal features on the badge of Chelsea FC?

ANSWERS

1. George Mackenzie
2. Colin Bell
3. 89
4. Nigel Worthington
5. Tottenham Hotspur
6. Bobby Charlton
7. 18
8. 1992
9. Mark Bowen
10. Lion

ROUND 9
SOCCER 15

QUESTIONS

1. In which year did Jock Stein manage Leeds United?
2. What animal features on the badge of Ipswich Town?
3. Who is Preston North End's most capped player?
4. When Aston Villa bought Gareth Southgate from Crystal Palace, how much did he cost?
5. Which country did Kevin Keegan play against in his last game for England?
6. For how much did Arsenal sign Ian Wright from Crystal Palace in 1991?
7. What animal features on the badge of Leicester City?
8. Which Celtic player was nicknamed 'The Flea'?
9. What year was Paul Ince born?
10. From which club did Joe Hulme join Blackburn in 1924?

ANSWERS

1. 1978
2. A horse
3. Tom Finney
4. £2.5m
5. Spain
6. £2.5m
7. A fox
8. Jimmy Johnstone
9. 1967
10. Hull City

ROUND 9
SOCCER 16

QUESTIONS

1. Which player scored the first goal of the 1994 FA Cup final?
2. For which country does Spurs striker Freddie Kanoute play?
3. Which Arsenal player was sent off twice in three days in the 2000/1 Premiership season?
4. Which Portuguese footballer became the Worlds most expensive player when he joined Real Madrid from Barcelona?
5. Which Everton player missed the penalty that led to France's Golden Goal victory over Portuagal at Euro 2000?
6. Which England International player became manager of Middlesborough in 1973?
7. Who did Scotland play against in the first match of the 1998 World Cup?
8. Who scored against France in 27 seconds in the 1982 World Cup?
9. Against whom did Arsenal secure the 97/98 Premiership title?
10. Which French footballer joined Aston Villa from Tottenham Hotspur in 2000?

ANSWERS

1. Teddy Sheringham
2. Mali
3. Patrick Viera
4. Luis Figo
5. Abel Xavier
6. Jack Charlton
7. Brazil
8. Bryan Robson
9. Everton
10. David Ginola

ROUND 10

SPORT

ROUND 10
SPORT 1

QUESTIONS

1. Russian gymnast Larisa Latynina holds the record for most Olympic medals. How many has she won?
2. Which horse won the Grand National in 1979?
3. Who won the British Open in 1982 and 1983?
4. What sport would you be playing with an foil?
5. What year was the Super Bowl first held?
6. Who was the first American football match under Harvard rules played between in 1874?
7. What is football also known as?
8. Who's nickname is the Crafty Cockney?
9. Which horse won the The Oaks in 1979?
10. What year was the first set of football rules drawn up at Cambridge University?

ANSWERS

1. 18 (9 gold medals, 5 silver medals and 4 bronze medals)
2. Rubstick
3. Tom Watson
4. Fencing
5. 1967
6. Harvard University and McGill University
7. Soccer
8. Eric Bristow
9. Scintillate
10. 1848

ROUND 10
SPORT 2

QUESTIONS

1. Who won the football World Cup in 1950?
2. How long is a round in boxing?
3. How many players are on a football team?
4. What is a golf ball hit from?
5. What year was the first cricket World Cup held?
6. How many points are scored when the yellow ball is potted in snooker?
7. What sport are The Oaks and St Leger related to?
8. What does PGA stand for?
9. In boxing what is the largest weight division know as?
10. In golf, what year was the first US Open first held?

ANSWERS

1. Uruguay
2. 3 minutes
3. Eleven
4. A tee
5. 1975
6. Two
7. Horse racing
8. Professional Golfers' Association
9. Heavyweight
10. 1895

ROUND 10
SPORT 3

QUESTIONS

1. How many players are there on a cricket team?
2. Fighting with gloves became standard in 1867 after the formulation of which set of rules?
3. What is the main piece in chess?
4. Where does Judo originate from?
5. The Refuge Assurance League and the Natwest Cup are championships in which game?
6. What year was the first Tour de France held?
7. In darts what is landing all three darts in the 1's know as?
8. On February 8th, 1983 which horse was kidnapped from Ballymany Stud?
9. In 1996, who lit the Olympic flame in Atlanta, Georgia?
10. The first modern Olympic Games were held in Athens, Greece in which year?

ANSWERS

1. Eleven
2. The Queensberry Rules
3. The King
4. Japan
5. Cricket
6. 1903
7. Bucket of nails
8. Shergar
9. Muhammad Ali
10. 1896

ROUND 10
SPORT 4

QUESTIONS

1. How many people are on a women's lacrosse team?
2. Which Brazilian racing driver was killed in a race on May 1, 1994?
3. In golf, what year was the first British Open first held?
4. What year was the first football World cup contested?
5. Which darts player was World Champion in 1980, 1981, 1984, 1985 and 1986?
6. As an Olympic sport what are the three main branches of equestrianism?
7. What year was the Football Association founded?
8. What year was the last bare knuckle fight?
9. How long is a cricket pitch?
10. Where is the British Showjumping Derby staged annually?

ANSWERS

1. Twelve
2. Ayrton Senna
3. 1860
4. 1930
5. Eric Bristow
6. Show jumping, three-day eventing and dressage.
7. 1863
8. 1889
9. 20m/22yds
10. Hickstead, Sussex

ROUND 10
SPORT 5

QUESTIONS

1. In darts what is a score of 45 otherwise know as?
2. What game might you use a 'flick serve'?
3. What year was the first baseball World Series held?
4. Who was the breeder of Shergar?
5. At the 1980 Olympics which country won at two man bobslieghing?
6. What game is played on a flat or crown green?
7. How many rounds does an Amateur round of boxing last?
8. What first became a Summer Olympic sport at the Barcelona Olympics in 1992?
9. What game according to tradition was invented in Cooperstown, New York by Abner Doubleday in 1839?
10. At the 1960 Summer Olympics in Rome, which boxer won a gold medal as a light heavyweight boxer?

ANSWERS

1. Bag o'nuts
2. Badminton
3. 1903
4. Aga Khan
5. Switzerland
6. Bowls
7. Three
8. Badminton
9. Baseball

Muhammad Ali

ROUND 10
SPORT 6

QUESTIONS

1. In 1975, who did Muhammad Ali defeat in the 'Thrilla in Manila'?
2. What year did Rome host the Olympic Games?
3. The high jump method of jumping head first and landing on the back is known as what?
4. In 1900, which city hosted the second Olympic Games?
5. Who won the BBC Sports Personality of the Year in December 2004?
6. Exactly how many stitches does a baseball have?
7. What sport has been played on the moon?
8. Which game was invented by William George Morgan of Holyoke, Massachusetts in 1895?
9. Which cricketer first played for Somerset at age 17?
10. When the first modern Olympic Games were held in Athens, Greece in 1896 how many male competitors were there?

ANSWERS

1. Joe Frazier
2. 1960
3. The Fosbury Flop
4. Paris
5. Kelly Holmes
6. 108 stitches
7. Golf. On 6th February 1971 Alan Shepard hit a golf ball
8. Volleyball
9. Ian Botham
10. 311

ROUND 10
SPORT 7

QUESTIONS

1. What are the four major international golf championships?
2. Which horse won the Grand National in 1980?
3. In 1891, James Naismith, a physical education instructor, introduced what sport?
4. Cassius Marcellus Clay Jr is otherwise know as who?
5. What game would you be playing if you shouted 'Fore'?
6. Which Briton won two medals in the 1960 Olympics for both the 100 metres and 200 metres?
7. Which sport was Victor Barna world champion five times?
8. Who lit the flame at the 1956 Olympics?
9. How many feathers on a standard shuttlecock?
10. What year was Matt Busby knighted?

ANSWERS

1. The British Open, The US open, the Masters and the United States PGA
2. Ben Nevis
3. Basketball
4. Muhammad Ali
5. Golf
6. Dorothy Hyman
7. Table tennis
8. Ron Clarke
9. Sixteen
10. 1968

ROUND 10
SPORT 8

QUESTIONS

1. In darts what is the number 1 otherwise known as?
2. Who rode Shergar to his 1981 Derby victory?
3. Who was Cassius Clay's first title fight against?
4. What is otherwise know as a 'cock', 'bird' or 'birdie'?
5. What year was the golf Masters first held?
6. Where was the 'Rumble in the Jungle'?
7. In darts how many points is the inner ring worth?
8. Who won the US Open in 1982?
9. In darts, what is the inner ring otherwise known as?
10. What year was the first official chess World Championship?

ANSWERS

1. Annie's Room
2. Walter Swinburn
3. Sonny Liston
4. A shuttlecock
5. 1934
6. Zaire
7. 50 points
8. Tom Watson
9. The Bull or Bullseye
10. 1886

ROUND 10
SPORT 9

QUESTIONS

1. What is the green fabric that covers a snooker table called?
2. Which horse won the Grand National in 1984?
3. In competitive swimming what are the four strokes?
4. How long is an Olympic sized pool?
5. How long does a World Championship or Olympic judo match last?
6. How many people are on a men's lacrosse team?
7. In skiing, who won the men's Alpine World cup in 1981, 82 and 83?
8. How many players on a Rugby League team?
9. Which snooker player is also known as 'The Whirlwind'?
10. What year was pairs skating introduced at the World Championships?

ANSWERS

1. Baize
2. Hallo Dandy
3. Freestyle, breaststroke, back-stroke and butterfly
4. 50 metres/ 55 yards long
5. 5 minutes
6. Ten
7. Phil Mahre
8. 13
9. Jimmy White
10. 1908

ROUND 10
SPORT 10

QUESTIONS

1. He holds the record for most gold medals won in a single Olympics (seven)?
2. What is the oldest and most prestigious event in the sport of tennis?
3. How many points are scored when the black ball is potted in snooker?
4. What date was the entire US figure skating team and their coaches killed in a plane crash in Brussels, en route to the World Championships in Prague?
5. What are the white cotton uniforms worn by judo players called?
6. What level is a white belt in Judo?
7. Which ball game was adopted form the North American Indians?
8. Which horse won the Grand National in 1983?
9. Who was the first men's singles champion at Wimbledon?
10. The WBC, WBA, IBF and the WBO are championships of which sport?

ANSWERS

1. Mark Spitz
2. Wimbledon
3. Seven
4. February 15, 1961
5. Judogi
6. Novice
7. Lacrosse
8. Corbiere
9. Spencer Gore
10. Boxing

ROUND 10
SPORT 11

QUESTIONS

1. How old was Ayrton Senna when he died in 1994?
2. In rowing what is the name for the propulsion of a boat by one rower with two oars?
3. What year was the first rowing World Championship held?
4. In golf what is the name of the grassed area between the tee and the green?
5. What belt is worn at the top level of proficiency in Judo?
6. Where does The Boat Race begin and end?
7. Torvill and Dean are famous for what?
8. Which racing driver has a sponsorship deal that will pay him US$8 million over three years for him to wear a four-inch ad on his post-race hat?
9. How many points are scored when a red ball is potted in snooker?
10. Where are the competitors of The Boat Race from?

ANSWERS

1. 34
2. Sculling
3. 1962
4. The Fairway
5. Black
6. From Putney to Mortlake. London
7. Ice dance
8. Michael Schumacher
9. One
10. The Oxford and Cambridge University rowing clubs

ROUND 10
SPORT 12

QUESTIONS

1. What is the professional form of Rugby football better known as?
2. Which sports event includes downhill, slalom and cross country racing?
3. The first televised maximum break of 147 was achieved in 1982 by whom?
4. Which figure skater set the fashion for female skaters to wear short skirts and white boots?
5. How many players on a Rugby Union team?
6. The Pilkington Cup is associated with which sport?
7. Which sport was founded by Jigoro Kano in 1882?
8. In which sport would you find salchows, lutzes and toe loops?
9. Biellman spins, where the skater pulls her free leg from behind her (or very rarely him), over the head, was named after which skating champion?
10. What year were the first championships held at Wimbledon?

ANSWERS

1. Rugby League
2. Skiing
3. Steve Davis
4. Sonja Henie
5. 15
6. Rugby
7. Judo
8. Figure skating
9. Denise Biellman
10. 1877

ROUND 10
SPORT 13

QUESTIONS

1. On October 30, 1974 who did Muhammad Ali defeat in "The Rumble in the Jungle"?
2. What year were the first basketball World Championships held?
3. Which country won the first basketball World Championships in 1950?
4. In the 1976 Olympics who was the most successful swimmer?
5. Which cricketer has scored the most runs for England in test matches?
6. In 1982, which Briton who was the World Freshwater Fishing champion?
7. Han Aiping of China was the 1985 and 1987 World Champion of what sport?
8. In which year were the Olympic Games first held in London?
9. What are the uprights of cricket wickets called?
10. In 1967 which boxer refused to serve in the American army during the Vietnam War as a conscientious objector?

ANSWERS

1. George Foreman
2. 1950
3. Argentina
4. David Wilkie
5. Geoffrey Boycott (8,114 in 108 tests)
6. Kevin Ashurst
7. Badminton
8. 1908
9. Stumps

Muhammad Ali

ROUND 10

SPORT 14

QUESTIONS

1. How many rounds does an Professional round of boxing last?
2. What year was the United States PGA first held?
3. What sport would you be playing with a sabre?
4. Which boxing promoter gained fame in 1974 by sponsoring the boxing match between Muhammad Ali and George Foreman in Zaire, popularly known as "The Rumble in the Jungle"?
5. In boxing what is the smallest weight division known as?   Mini-flyweight or paperweight.
6. In darts what is the highest score possible from 3 darts?
7. What game would you be playing with 2 players, 16 pieces each and a board of 64 squares of alternating colour?
8. What year did Mike Tyson first become WBC/ WBA World Heavyweight Boxing champion?
9. In Judo, how many degrees does a black belt signify?
10. The Boat Race was first held in which year?

ANSWERS

1. Twelve
2. 1916
3. Fencing
4. Don King
5. Under 49kg/108lb
6. 180
7. Chess
8. 1986
9. Nine
10. 1829

ROUND 10
SPORT 15

QUESTIONS

1. Which horse won The Derby in 1981?
2. Who is statistically the most successful F1 driver ever, with the most career victories, and a record seven world driver championships?
3. In 1988 which figure skater was credited with completing the first quadruple jump in competition?
4. What is the amateur form of Rugby football better known as?
5. Which snooker player won the World Championships 15 consecutive times from 1927 to 1946?
6. In which sport are degrees of proficiency indicated with a coloured belt?
7. Who won the football World Cup in 1966?
8. How many holes do most golf courses have?
9. Which horse won the Grand National in 1986?
10. Which snooker champion is nicknamed 'The Nugget'?

ANSWERS

1. Shergar
2. Michael Schumacher
3. Kurt Browning
4. Rugby Union
5. Joe Davis (England)
6. Judo
7. England
8. Eighteen
9. West Tip
10. Steve Davis

ROUND 10
SPORT 16

QUESTIONS

1. Which country won the 1969 lacrosse World Championships?
2. In 1894 where was the first motor race held?
3. Which boxer has been champion at five different weights?
4. What year was Shergar born?
5. During the Swedish Open in the summer of 1987, which darts player found himself unable to let go of his darts properly - a psychological condition known as 'dartitis'?
6. What belt is worn after examination in Judo?
7. Which glamorous figure skater took the gold medal in the 1928, 1932 and 1936 Winter Olympics?
8. Which racing driver earns an estimated US$80 million annually, including all of his endorsement deals?
9. Who won the first cricket World Cup?
10. Who won the football World Cup in 1958,1962 and 1970?

ANSWERS

1. Great Britain
2. Paris
3. Sugar Ray Leonard
4. 1978
5. Eric Bristow
6. Brown
7. Sonja Henie
8. Michael Schumacher
9. West Indies
10. Brazil

ROUND 10
SPORT 17

QUESTIONS

1. Who was the first woman to finish in the Grand National?
2. Which position did English soccer star Stanley Matthews play?
3. In which game would you use a tee?
4. In which game would you use a foil?
5. In which sport was Darrell Pace the 1979 world champion?
6. What year did the Badminton World Championships begin?
7. The Thomas Cup and the Uber Cup are competitions for which sport?
8. What illness was Muhammad Ali diagnosed with in 1982?
9. Where were the 1984 Olympics held?
10. What is the national summer game of the USA?

ANSWERS

1. Geraldine Rees in 1982
2. Outside right
3. Golf
4. Fencing
5. Archery
6. 1977
7. Badminton
8. Pugilistic Parkinson's syndrome
9. Los Angeles
10. Baseball

ROUND 10
SPORT 18

QUESTIONS

1. What year was the first Grand National held?
2. What does FIFA stand for?
3. Who is considered to be the most successful Olympic athlete in the history of the modern Olympics?
4. Since what year has fencing been part of the Olympic program?
5. What is the oldest English horse race?
6. What is the world's biggest participant sport?
7. When the first modern Olympic Games were held in Athens, Greece in 1896 how many female competitors were there?
8. What is the most attended or watched sport in the world?
9. What year did boxing become a legal sport?
10. What game is 'arrows' slang for?

ANSWERS

1. 1836
2. Federation Internationale de Football Association
3. Ray Ewry
4. 1896
5. St Leger, began 1776
6. Fishing
7. None
8. Football
9. 1901
10. Darts

ROUND 11
TECHNOLOGY & INVENTIONS

ROUND 11
TECHNOLOGY & INVENTIONS 1

QUESTIONS

1. Who invented nylon in 1935?
2. What year did Earl Silas Tupper patent the Tupperware seal?
3. Who invented Velcro ®?
4. Who invented the Wurlitzer jukebox?
5. Ralph Schneider introduced the world to what in 1950?
6. In 1956, Bette Nesmith Graham invented what?
7. Who invented the air conditioner in 1903?
8. What year did James Russell invent the compact disc?
9. Alan Shugart invented what in 1970?
10. Arthur Fry invented what in 1974?

ANSWERS

1. Wallace Carothers
2. 1947
3. George de Mestral
4. Robert Hope-Jones
5. The credit card
6. Tipp-Ex®
7. Willis Carrier
8. 1965
9. The floppy disk
10. The Post-It® note

ROUND 11
TECHNOLOGY & INVENTIONS 2

QUESTIONS

1. Mary Phelps Jacob invented what in 1913?
2. Gideon Sundback invented which fastener?
3. What year did Eugene Sullivan and William Taylor develop Pyrex® glass in New York City?
4. What was invented by Percy Spencer in 1946?
5. What pastime did Walter Frederick Morrison and Warren Franscioni invent in 1948?
6. In 1920 who invented the Band-Aid?
7. What year was Technicolor invented?
8. What sticky product did Walter E. Diemer invent in 1928?
9. What did Edwin Herbert Land invent?
10. Which Englishmen invented cat eyes or roads reflectors in 1934?

ANSWERS

1. The Bra
2. The zip
3. 1915
4. The microwave oven
5. The Frisbee®
6. Earle Dickson
7. 1927
8. Bubble gum
9. Polaroid photography
10. Percy Shaw

ROUND 11
TECHNOLOGY & INVENTIONS 3

QUESTIONS

1. Who built the first train to be powered by locomotion, on 27 September 1825?
2. Whose invention is credited with starting the 'Industrial Revolution'?
3. Who designed the 'Catch Me Who Can'?
4. When was Isambard Kingdom Brunel's Great Eastern ship launched?
5. The Great Eastern was designed to sail from England to where?
6. What was the first public steam railway in the world?
7. What is the 'Chunnel' otherwise known as?
8. Who was Puffing Billy designed by?
9. Who designed the Davy lamp in1816 to assist miners?
10. What year was inventor Thomas Alva Edison born?

ANSWERS

1. Robert Stephenson & Co
2. Richard Arkwright
3. Richard Trevithick
4. 1858
5. Australia
6. The Stockton and Darlington Railway
7. The Channel Tunnel
8. William Hedley
9. Sir Humphry Davy
10. 1847

ROUND 11
TECHNOLOGY & INVENTIONS 4

QUESTIONS

1. Ladislo Biro invented what in1938?
2. Who invented the zeppelin?
3. Who invented the double-edged safety razor?
4. What did Mary Anderson invent in 1904?
5. Teabags invented in 1904 by who?
6. What year did Albert Einstein publish 'The Theory of Relativity'?
7. What did William Kellogg invent in1906?
8. What year did Leo Baekeland invent?
9. What did Jacques E. Brandenberger invent?
10. What beverage did G. Washington invent?

ANSWERS

1. The ballpoint pen
2. Count Ferdinand von Zeppelin
3. King Camp Gillette
4. Windscreen wipers
5. Thomas Sullivan
6. 1905
7. Cornflakes
8. Bakelite
9. Cellophane
10. Instant coffee

ROUND 11
TECHNOLOGY & INVENTIONS 5

QUESTIONS

1. What mode of transportation were pneumatic tyres originally invented for?
2. What was invented by Norwegian Johann Vaale?
3. What year was music first sent down a telephone line?
4. The can opener was invented how many years after cans were introduced?
5. When Edison died in 1931, how many patents for the telephone did he own?
6. What year was the first neon sign made?
7. What year was the first fax process patented?
8. What game was invented by Charles Darrow in 1933?
9. Who was an hour behind Alexander Graham Bell's patenting pf his telephone?
10. Who invented the 'Dyson' vacuum cleaner?

ANSWERS

1. Bicycles
2. The paperclip
3. 1876
4. 48 years
5. 34
6. 1923
7. 1843
8. Monopoly
9. Elisha Grey
10. James Dyson

ROUND 11
TECHNOLOGY & INVENTIONS 6

QUESTIONS

1. What did Karl Ludwig Nessler of Germany invent in 1906?
2. How many patents did Thomas Edison file?
3. When Edison died in 1931, how many patents for electric light and power did he own?
4. What did Count Alessandro Volta invent in the 18th century?
5. Who developed the world's first photographic image in 1827?
6. In 1894, what did Thomas Edison and W K L Dickson introduce?
7. What was sent in 1972 by Ray Tomlinson?
8. Who's was idea was it to use the @ sign to separate the name of the user from the name of the computer?
9. A semi-mechanical analogue television system was first demonstrated in London in February 1924 with an image of what?
10. In 1936 how many TV sets were there in the world?

ANSWERS

1. The permanent wave or "hair perm"
2. 1,093
3. 389
4. The first battery
5. Joseph Niepce
6. The first film camera
7. The first electronic mail, or "email"
8. Ray Tomlinson
9. Felix the Cat
10. 100

ROUND 11
TECHNOLOGY & INVENTIONS 7

QUESTIONS

1. What did Giorgio Fischer, a Italian gynaecologist, invent?
2. What was the Great Eastern known as before its launch?
3. What year was the human growth hormone genetically engineered?
4. Where was the first projected film to a paying audience shown?
5. When was the Windows program invented by Microsoft?
6. What year did the first railway locomotive run?
7. Who constructed the world's first steam railway locomotive?
8. Where was Robert Louis Stevenson born?
9. What year were disposable contact lenses invented?
10. How many men lost their lives during construction of the Forth Bridge in Scotland?

ANSWERS

1. Liposuction
2. The Leviathan
3. 1982
4. Grand Café, Paris, December 1895
5. 1985
6. 1803
7. George Stephenson
8. Edinburgh Scotland
9. 1987
10. 57

ROUND 11
TECHNOLOGY & INVENTIONS 8

QUESTIONS

1. What was the name of the last steam locomotive built by British Rail?
2. Who invented the Model T car?
3. What year was the last steam locomotive removed from use in America?
4. The brothers Louis and Auguste Lumière patented what in 1895?
5. What year was the Forth Bridge completed?
6. In 1990, who created The World Wide Web/Internet?
7. When were the first electric lights installed in New York?
8. What was designed by J. K. Starley of Coventry and was first exhibited in London in 1885?
9. In what year did Albert Matthieu-Favier, a French engineer put forward the first proposal for the a Channel Tunnel?
10. In 1866, which ship was used to lay the first successful transatlantic telegraph cable linking Britain and America?

ANSWERS

1. Evening Star
2. Henry Ford
3. 1960
4. Their cinématographe device
5. 1890
6. Tim Berners-Lee
7. 1882
8. The Rover safety bicycle. Rover eventually became an automobile brand.
9. 1802
10. The Great Eastern

ROUND 11
TECHNOLOGY & INVENTIONS 9

QUESTIONS

1. What year was the iconic iMac introduced?
2. The first atomic bomb test explosion was equivalent to how many tonnes of conventional high explosive?
3. What did Albert Einstein come to regard it as 'the greatest mistake' of his life?
4. Who developed the first photographic negatives from which multiple prints could be made?
5. What year did the first public telegraph service begin?
6. What year saw the first public demonstration of Morse's electric telegraph from Baltimore to Washington?
7. Who invented the first workable photographic process?
8. Who, before Singer developed the first really practical machine that could sew?
9. Which ad impresario coined the word 'sneaker' for sports shoes?
10. Who invented the shower proof coat in 1823?

ANSWERS

1. 1998
2. 19,000 tonnes
3. His work on the Atomic Bomb
4. William Henry Fox Talbot
5. 1839
6. 1844
7. Louis Daguerre
8. Elias Howe
9. Henry McKinney
10. Charles Macintosh

ROUND 11
TECHNOLOGY & INVENTIONS 10

QUESTIONS

1. The first ever TV interview – featuring Irish actress Peggy O'Neil – was conducted in what year?
2. What was started by the BBC in November 1936?
3. Who designed the first watch to go into space?
4. What was invented by the Ampex corporation of California in 1956?
5. What was the Ampex VR1000?
6. The home video recorder was introduced by Philips of the Netherlands in which year?
7. Which Japanese company introduced the VHS system in 1976?
8. What year was the Hubble Space telescope lauched into orbit by the US space shuttle?
9. What is a set of interconnected computer networks that are connected by internetworking better known as?
10. What is WI-FI short for?

ANSWERS

1. 1930
2. The first daily television broadcast
3. Bulova
4. The video recording machine
5. The first video recorder
6. 1972
7. JVC
8. 1990
9. The Internet
10. Wireless Fidelity

ROUND 11
TECHNOLOGY & INVENTIONS 11

QUESTIONS

1. What was the nickname of the first nuclear bomb to be exploded in tests?
2. How far away from the first atomic explosion was the heat felt by witnesses?
3. What year was the plastic Barbie doll made by Mattel, introduced?
4. What was the first Kodak camera to be designed and built in Britain?
5. What year was Prozac first released?
6. What year was Viagra released?
7. What did Mahatma Gandhi declare, 'was one of the few useful things ever invented'?
8. What did Polaroid's introduce in 1962?
9. What year was the first Atlantic telegraph cable completed?
10. What did Edwin Budding invent?

ANSWERS

1. Gadget
2. Ten miles
3. 1959
4. Kodak 'Six-20 Brownie C' roll film box camera
5. 1987
6. 1998
7. The sewing machine
8. Instant colour pictures
9. 1858
10. The first lawnmower

ROUND 11
TECHNOLOGY & INVENTIONS 12

QUESTIONS

1. What year was the design for the Model T first introduced?
2. JET 1 was the world's first gas turbine-powered motor car, who was it made by?
3. Who masterminded the Atom Bomb?
4. Who invented the rolling production line?
5. How long did the Forth Bridge take to build?
6. What is the second longest rail tunnel in the World?
7. When did the first V2 missile fall on London?
8. What is Caltech short for?
9. At the outbreak of the First World War which country was world leader in bicycle exports?
10. What year did the world's first regular high-definition television service begin?

ANSWERS

1. 1908
2. Rover
3. Robert Oppenheimer
4. Henry Ford
5. Seven years
6. The Channel Tunnel
7. 8 September 1944
8. California Institute of Technology
9. Britain
10. 1936

ROUND 11
TECHNOLOGY & INVENTIONS 13

QUESTIONS

1. On 6th August 1945, what weapon was first used in combat?
2. How many days after Hiroshima before the second Atomic Bomb was dropped on Nagasaki?
3. In 1965, what percentage of the US federal budget was spent on the Apollo 10?
4. What year was the Model T finally phased out?
5. Which NASA project took 500 million man hours to complete?
6. Tom Stafford, John Young and Gene Cernan travelled where in 1969?
7. What year was Greenwich time made the standard for Britain?
8. 1976 what did Steve Wozniak, Steven Jobs and Ron Wayne devise?
9. Which computer established the market for personal computers?
10. What is the name of Britain's most successful solar-powered racing car?

ANSWERS

1. The atomic bomb
2. Three days
3. Over 5%
4. 1927
5. Apollo 10
6. Around the moon
7. 1880
8. The Apple I computer
9. Apple II
10. Mad Dog

ROUND 11
TECHNOLOGY & INVENTIONS 14

QUESTIONS

1. Henry Ford's massive Highland Park plant was in which US city?
2. What was the most common aircraft During the First World War?
3. How many V2 missiles hit England during WW2?
4. The inventor of Tipp-Ex®'s son was in a pop band. Which one?
5. How long is the Channel Tunnel?
6. When was John Logie Baird born?
7. Computer Space was the first what?
8. What year was the Apple II launched?
9. Which newly completed bridge in 1890 had the largest span?
10. What was the Atom bomb development programme's codename?

ANSWERS

1. Detroit
2. The Avro 504
3. 1,100
4. The Monkees
5. 50km
6. 13 August 1888
7. Arcade video game
8. 1977
9. The Forth Bridge
10. The Manhattan Project

ROUND 11
TECHNOLOGY & INVENTIONS 15

QUESTIONS

1. What was the Trinity project?
2. Who was the first person to televise an image using mechanical scanning?
3. What year was the British Broadcasting Company (BBC) set up?
4. The first electric typewriter was introduced in which year?
5. Who piloted the plane that dropped the world's first atomic bomb on Hiroshima?
6. What year was Meccano introduced?
7. What year was the Kodak 'Six-20 Brownie C' roll film box camera introduced?
8. When was the first demonstration of true television?
9. What year did Peter Goldmark of Columbia Records launch the first successful microgroove vinyl LPs?
10. When was the Nintendo 'Game Boy' introduced?

ANSWERS

1. The first atomic test
2. John Logie Baird
3. 1922
4. 1947
5. Paul Tibbets Jr
6. 1901
7. 1948
8. 27 January 1926
9. 1948
10. 1989

ROUND 11
TECHNOLOGY & INVENTIONS 16

QUESTIONS

1. Jacques Cousteau invented SCUBA and Albert Hoffman LSD in the same year, which year?
2. Where is the tallest building in the USA?
3. How many Ford Model T cars were produced before being phased out?
4. What was the name of the first car imported into Britain in 1895?
5. Cyborg is a contraction of which two words?
6. How much explosive amatol did a V2 missile carry?
7. What date was the atomic bomb dropped on Hiroshima?
8. What did William Shockley, Walter Brattain, and John Bardeen develop in 1948?
9. In computing what does NAND stand for?
10. In 1919, Fords accounted for what percentage of vehicles on British roads?

ANSWERS

1. 1943
2. Chicago (Sears Tower)
3. 15 million
4. Panhard & Levassor
5. Cybernetic and orgnism
6. 1000 kg (2204 lb)
7. 6 August 1945
8. The transistor
9. Not and
10. 40%

ROUND 11
TECHNOLOGY & INVENTIONS 17

QUESTIONS

1. What was the name of Craig Breedlove's record-breaking jet car?
2. In 1914, Henry Ford made the decision to paint all his cars what colour?
3. What nationality was Marie Curie?
4. What year did Edward Jenner start vaccination?
5. What did Guglielmo Marconi demonstrate in December 1903?
6. What year was the Goblin automatic tea-maker patented?
7. What was the name of the aircraft that dropped the bomb on Hiroshima?
8. In 1927 what was transmitted over 700 km (435 miles) of telephone lines between London and Glasgow?
9. What was the first mass-marketed men's hair care product?
10. What year was penicillin eventually isolated?

ANSWERS

1. Spirit of America
2. Black
3. Polish (though she was bred in France)
4. 1796
5. That radio waves could span the Atlantic
6. 1934
7. Enola Gay
8. Television
9. Brylcreem
10. 1939

ROUND 11
TECHNOLOGY & INVENTIONS 18

QUESTIONS

1. What year was colour television first demonstrated?
2. What did Isaac Merritt Singer (1811-1875) design in 1850?
3. In February 1936, what did Hungarian physicist Leo Szilard donate the British War Office the patent to?
4. What date was the BBC's first broadcast in London?
5. What year was the first vacuum tube hearing aid developed which contained the battery inside?
6. What was invented by W H Brenner Thornton and William Hermannfirst?
7. Which watch manufacturer sold Sinclair computers in the USA under its own brand?
8. What year did John Logie Baird die?
9. Which eminent scientist worked on the atomic bomb with Leo Szilard?
10. What kitchen appliance business did Ken Wood launch in 1947?

ANSWERS

1. 1948
2. Sewing machine
3. The atomic bomb
4. 14 November 1922
5. 1944
6. The Goblin Teasmade
7. Timex
8. 1946
9. Albert Einstein
10. Kenwood Chef food mixer

ROUND 12 ANIMALS

ROUND 12
ANIMALS 1

QUESTIONS

1. What is the average lifespan of a gerbil?
2. How long were the tentacles of the largest recorded captured giant squid?
3. Feline is the descriptive term for which animal?
4. What is a female giraffe called?
5. What country do Budgerigars originate?
6. Who many kilos of meat can lions can eat in a single meal?
7. What are the only British bird of prey to feed exclusively on fish?
8. What is a group of deer called?
9. What are marsupials?
10. How many nesting pairs of Ospreys does Scotland have?

ANSWERS

1. 3 years
2. 10 m (35 ft) long
3. Cats
4. A cow
5. Australia
6. 40 kg
7. Ospreys
8. A herd
9. Animals which nurture their babies in pouches
10. 130

ROUND 12
ANIMALS 2

QUESTIONS

1. Lions live up to 20 years in the wild in a social structure known as what?
2. The female of which species stand on their hind legs and 'box' advancing males?
3. What is a baby bear called?
4. What kind of owls allow blind snakes to live in their nests?
5. Insects outnumber humans by how many?
6. What is a group of giraffes called?
7. How many Chimpanzees are there alive in the wild?
8. How close do cheetahs get to their prey before giving chase?
9. What insect lives in colonies?
10. Red kangaroos are Australia's largest what?

ANSWERS

1. A pride
2. Hares
3. A cub
4. Screech
5. 200 million to one.
6. A tower or a herd
7. 150,000
8. 10-30m
9. Wasps
10. Marsupial

ROUND 12
ANIMALS 3

QUESTIONS

1. Cats belong to which mammal family order?
2. Which animal has the most powerful jaws on the planet?
3. What is the oldest breed of dog?
4. What did the largest giant squid ever recorded captured weigh?
5. What is the smallest bird in the world?
6. What is the top speed an ostrich can run?
7. What is the world's smallest dog?
8. What is a male bear called?
9. What are the smallest crabs in the world?
10. 75% of wild birds die before they are how old?

ANSWERS

1. Felidae
2. Sharks
3. The Saluki
4. 4 tons
5. The bee hummingbird of Cuba
6. Up to 70 km/h (43mph).
7. The Chihuahua
8. A boar
9. Pea crabs (the size of a pea)
10. 6 months old

ROUND 12
ANIMALS 4

QUESTIONS

1. What is a female kangaroo called?
2. Apart from man, what is the jaguar's biggest threat?
3. Which breed of bark-less African dog is depicted on the walls of Egyptian tombs?
4. Grey squirrels introduced from America now outnumber Britain's native red squirrel by how many?
5. What type of silk is stronger and more flexible than steel?
6. What is a group of penguins called?
7. Which animals have a constant body temperature like mammals but lay eggs like reptiles? .
8. Which animals bite the base of each other's tail forming a daisy chain to avoid being separated?
9. Horned lizards spray blood from which part of its body when faced with a predator?
10. How may humps has the Dromedary camel?

ANSWERS

1. A flyer
2. Anaconda
3. The Basenji Hound
4. Fifteen to one
5. Spider silk
6. A colony or a parade
7. Birds
8. Families of Asian shrews
9. Its eyes
10. One

ROUND 12
ANIMALS 5

QUESTIONS

1. What creature is the fastest swimmer, reaching 109 km/h (68 mph)?
2. What is the slowest fish?
3. In Denmark there are twice as many what as people?
4. What swimming speeds can Dolphins reach?
5. How many times stronger than a human's bite is a shark's?
6. How many types of leeches are there?
7. Which animal's tongue is as long as an elephant?
8. What is a male dolphin called?
9. What is the name of the MGM lion mascot?
10. Which animal's tongue is attached to the roof of its mouth and cannot be moved?

ANSWERS

1. The sailfish
2. The Sea Horse, which moves along at about 0.016 km/h (0.01 mph).
3. Pigs
4. 60 km/h (37 mph)
5. A hundred times
6. 650
7. The blue whale
8. A bull
9. Leo
10. A crocodile's

ROUND 12
ANIMALS 6

QUESTIONS

1. What is a group of bears called?
2. Big cats aim for what part of body for a kill?
3. Which animals are descended from early carnivores called miacids?
4. What is the name for birds of prey which catch their food with their claws?
5. What animal has an upper lip that is split in two with each part separately mobile?
6. How many times better than a human can a domestic cat hear?
7. What is a female fox called?
8. How many times stronger than a human's is a domestic cat's sense of smell?
9. Which dog is also known as the Persian Greyhound?
10. How many litres of milk per day does a nursing blue whale mothers produce?

ANSWERS

1. A sloth or a pack
2. Throat
3. All cats
4. Raptors
5. A camel
6. Three
7. A vixen
8. 14
9. The Saluki
10. Over 200

ROUND 12
ANIMALS 7

QUESTIONS

1. Lupine is the descriptive term for which animal?
2. Which animal has a heart the size of a small car?
3. How many times are Pigs mentioned in the Bible?
4. A Vulture's sense of smell is so refined that it can smell a rotting carcass from how many miles away?
5. What is a group of geese in the air?
6. How many million years have Sharks been roaming the oceans?
7. What are the world's fastest animals?
8. What is a male penguin called?
9. How long have felids been on the evolutionary timeline?
10. What are the largest predators on land?

ANSWERS

1. Wolves
2. The blue whale
3. Twice
4. 25 miles
5. A skein
6. 400
7. Peregrine falcons
8. A sire
9. 40 million
10. Polar Bears

ROUND 12
ANIMALS 8

QUESTIONS

1. Which monkey can swim under water distances of up to 20 metres?
2. What substance are the scales of a crocodile made of?
3. What is the most numerous bird species?
4. What are the only animals with flaps around the ears?
5. How many teeth do African elephants have to chew their food with?
6. How long does a house fly live?
7. What is a male giraffe called?
8. Which monkeys have the largest noses of any primate?
9. Which was the first animal in space?
10. What is the only animal that hunts humans?

ANSWERS

1. Proboscis monkeys
2. Ceratin
3. The red-billed quelea of southern Africa. There are an estimated 100 trillion of them.
4. Mammals.
5. Four
6. 14 days
7. A bull
8. Proboscis monkeys
9. A dog
10. Polar Bear

ROUND 12
ANIMALS 9

QUESTIONS

1. Which cats are the common ancestor of all pet cats?
2. During World War 2 the British military ordered the destruction of which bird to stop them killing government carrier pigeons?
3. Which animals skin has long been used as sandpaper?
4. How long was the largest recorded blue shark?
5. Which animals can catch food with sticks, and even like to dance in the rain?
6. What are the only cats to have manes?
7. The mule is the result of cross breeding which two animals?
8. What is a female penguin called?
9. The male of the cat family is almost twice the size of a female?
10. What bird swims deeper than any other?

ANSWERS

1. Wildcats
2. Peregrine falcons
3. Sharks
4. 3.83m
5. Chimpanzees
6. Male lions
7. A Male donkey with a female horse
8. A dam
9. Leopard
10. Emperor penguins

ROUND 12
ANIMALS 10

QUESTIONS

1. Which animal is rated the fourth most intelligent?
2. How many times are Sheep mentioned in the Bible?
3. What is the world's most widely-eaten meat?
4. The coyote is a member of the what animal family?
5. Which animal can clean its ears with its 50cm (20 in) tongue?
6. What is a male deer called?
7. The critically endangered Iberian Lynx is a native of which country?
8. What is a group of geese on the ground?
9. Which animal eats more than 30,000 ants a day?
10. Which animal can reach swimming speeds of 70 km/h (44 mph)?

ANSWERS

1. The pig
2. 45 times
3. Pork
4. Dogs
5. A giraffe
6. A buck
7. Spain
8. A gaggle
9. The South American giant anteater
10. Shark

ROUND 12
ANIMALS 11

QUESTIONS

1. Which animal plays dead when faced with a predator, keeling over and releasing a convincing smell of rotting flesh?
2. What are our closest relatives?
3. Black panthers are actually what?
4. Which fish is one of the most poisonous creatures in the sea, and a dangerous delicacy in Japan?
5. What is a baby deer called?
6. How many times are goats mentioned in the Bible?
7. Why do toads inflate their bodies when threatened?
8. What is a group of foxes called?
9. What animal fires secretions out of their anal glands when threatened. The smell is strong enough to induce vomiting?
10. By what year was the Tasmanian tiger extinct?

ANSWERS

1. Possum
2. Chimpanzees
3. Melanistic jaguars. They are an occasional anomaly in ordinary jaguar litters
4. The puffer fish
5. A fawn
6. 88 times
7. To convince predators that they are too big to swallow
8. A pack or a skulk
9. Skunks
10. 1930

ROUND 12
ANIMALS 12

QUESTIONS

1. How many of the eight tiger species have disappeared in the last fifty years?
2. In the 1700s, which birds were hunted almost to extinction for their feathers?
3. What is a group of swans called?
4. Which male tiger is the biggest and most powerful member of the entire cat family?
5. Which nation of 17 million people has more than 150 million sheep?
6. What is a baby swan called?
7. Which insect can carry 10 times their body weight?
8. Measured in straight flight, what is the fastest bird?
9. Canine is the descriptive term for which animal?
10. Which dog food salesman was the founder of Crufts dog show?

ANSWERS

1. Three
2. Ostriches
3. A wedge or a herd
4. Siberian, it measures up to 4m long and weighs more than 300kg
5. Australia
6. A cygnet
7. The worker ant
8. The tailed swift, it flies 170 km/h (106 mph)
9. Dog
10. Charles Cruft

ROUND 12
ANIMALS 13

QUESTIONS

1. On average, how many litters do female gerbils produce?
2. How many offspring does a female gerbil produce in a lifetime, on average?
3. Porcine is the descriptive term for which animal?
4. Tyzzer's Disease affects Gerbils, the symptoms include tiredness, lack of appetite and what?
5. What are the most popular species of pet bird?
6. How many words can a Minah birds remember?
7. What is a female swan called?
8. The MGM lion logo was originally created in 1916 by which advertising executive?
9. Which bird can imitate other animals and even human voices?
10. What is a male monkey called?

ANSWERS

1. Seven
2. 42
3. Pig
4. Diarrhoea.
5. Budgerigars
6. Two Hundred plus
7. A pen
8. Howard Dietz
9. Crows
10. A father

ROUND 12
ANIMALS 14

QUESTIONS

1. Which creatures do not have eyelids - their eyes are protected by a hardened lens?
2. What animal is also know as an earth pig?
3. Equine is the descriptive term for which animal?
4. What is a baby monkey called?
5. What year was the last time a rare white tiger was seen in the wild?
6. Are Polar Bears left or right handed?
7. How many types of pure breed dogs are there?
8. What is a group of kangaroos called?
9. What European city is said to have more dogs than people?
10. What was the name of the chimpanzee who starred in the original 1930s to 40s Tarzan movies starring JohnnyWeissmuller?

ANSWERS

1. Fish and insects
2. Aardvark
3. Horse
4. An infant
5. 1951
6. Left
7. 701
8. A troop, mob or herd
9. Paris
10. Cheeta

ROUND 12
ANIMALS 15

QUESTIONS

1. What is a female monkey called?
2. What is a puma also known as?
3. What are the largest living birds?
4. What has the loudest call of all animals?
5. Which animals enabled doctors to determine different blood groups in humans?
6. Which were the first primates in space?
7. What is a group of dolphins called?
8. What are the largest penguins?
9. What animal can outrun any other on earth?
10. What are the fastest land animals in the UK?

ANSWERS

1. A mother
2. A cougar
3. Ostriches
4. South America's Howler monkeys can carry their voices for more than 1.6km
5. Rhesus monkeys
6. Rhesus monkeys
7. A school or a pod
8. Emperor penguins
9. Cheetahs
10. Brown hares, they can reach speeds of 70km/h to avoid predators

ROUND 12
ANIMALS 16

QUESTIONS

1. How many pairs of tentacles does a snail have?
2. What was the heaviest crustacean ever found?
3. What is a female sheep called?
4. What length were the tentacles of the largest jellyfish ever caught?
5. What colour is squid ink?
6. What has the biggest eyes of any animal?
7. Which animals are immune to all known diseases?
8. The small tooth-like spikes on a sharks skin are called what?
9. What is a male kangaroo called?
10. What year did the MGM lion mascot first appear animated?

ANSWERS

1. Two
2. A lobster weighing 19 kg (42 lb). caught in 1934
3. A ewe
4. 36m (120 ft) long
5. Black
6. The giant squid, its eyes measure 40 cm (16 in) in diameter
7. Sharks.
8. Denticles
9. A boomer
10. 1924

ROUND 13

SHOPS

SHOPPING

ROUND 13
SHOPS & SHOPPING 1

QUESTIONS

1. Which London store was bought by the al-Fayed brothers in 1985?
2. What is the name of the Art Deco department store on Park Avenue, New York?
3. What does the London store Hamleys sell?
4. What does Agent Provocateur sell?
5. What does HMV stand for?
6. What is Jimmy Choo famous for?
7. What is Monolo Blahnik famous for?
8. What was the first supermarket chain to use shopping trolleys?
9. Agent Provocateur owner Joseph Corre is the son of which famous fashion designer?
10. What is New York's most famous toy shop?

ANSWERS

1. Harrods
2. Bloomingdales
3. Toys
4. Lingerie
5. His Master's Voice
6. Shoes
7. Ladies shoes
8. Piggly Wiggly
9. Vivienne Westwood
10. FAO Schwarz

ROUND 13
SHOPS & SHOPPING 2

QUESTIONS

1. Which company bought Harrods In 1959?
2. Which fashion designer was fatally stabbed by his lover Diego Cogolato in 1996?
3. What year was the first Tesco self-service store opened in St Albans?
4. What year was the first Tesco 'Supermarket' opened?
5. Which is the most expensive street in the world to rent retail space?
6. What is the largest menswear store in the world?
7. Which jeweler was sacked for disparaging remarks about his own company?
8. What does Ryman specialize in?
9. When was the trademark Burberry check first used?
10. What are Kellogs best known for?

1. House of Fraser
2. Ossie Clark
3. 1948
4. 1956
5. Fifth Avenue, New York
6. Slaters in Glasgow
7. George Ratner
8. Stationery
9. 1924
10. Breakfast cereals

ROUND 13
SHOPS & SHOPPING 3

QUESTIONS

1. What does the London shop Angels and Bermans specialize in?
2. What college did Ossie Clark secure his first class degree at?
3. James Smith and Son of New Oxford St London sells what?
4. What year did James Smith and Son of London first open?
5. Which Scottish menswear store covers 2,600 square meters?
6. What happened in Harrods on December 17, 1983?
7. Which New York store is often cheekily referred to as 'Needless Mark-up'?
8. What online auction site has 135 million registered users worldwide?
9. Where did the tea trade originate?
10. In 1609, John Rolfe arrived at the Jamestown Settlement in Virginia to grow the first crop of what?

ANSWERS

1. Costume Hire
2. The Royal College of Art
3. Umbrellas and walking sticks
4. 1830
5. Slaters
6. A car bomb killed six people and injured 90
7. Neiman Marcus
8. eBay
9. China
10. Tobacco leaf

ROUND 13
SHOPS & SHOPPING 4

QUESTIONS

1. What year did Wrangler introduced their 'western jean'?
2. Doc Martens was the brainchild of whom?
3. Which English shoe company produced the popular 'wallabee' in the 1950s?
4. What year was Gucci founded?
5. Where does Harris tweed come from?
6. Created in 1902, the fragrance 'Blenheim Bouquet' is made by which English perfume company?
7. What is Jo Malone famous for?
8. What is TopShop's customer profile age?
9. Which English luxury leather goods company was established by Roger Saul in the 1970s in rural Somerset?
10. What country does designer brand Prada hail from?

ANSWERS

1. 1947
2. Dr Klaus Maertens
3. Clarks
4. 1923
5. The island of Harris in Scotland
6. Penhaligons
7. Fragrance and skincare products
8. 16-34
9. Mulberry
10. Italy

ROUND 13
SHOPS & SHOPPING 5

QUESTIONS

1. Who invented nylon?
2. Where did the Nike company get their name from?
3. What year did Louis Vuitton start his luggage business?
4. In 1971, designer, Carolyn Davidson, was paid how much for her Nike Swoosh logo?
5. Which town in England was Reebok founded?
6. What is the French term for 'high sewing'?
7. Which swinging 60s London fashion store was the brainchild of Barbara Hulanicki?
8. What is the famous LA store based on Melrose Avenue in Hollywood?
9. Which New York store did Barney Pressman open in 1923?
10. What would you buy in Steinberg and Tolkein?

ANSWERS

1. Wallace Caruthers
2. The Greek goddess of victory
3. 1854
4. $35
5. Bolton in Lancashire
6. Haute Couture
7. Biba
8. Fred Segal
9. Barneys
10. Vintage clothing and accessories

ROUND 13
SHOPS & SHOPPING 6

QUESTIONS

1. In 1979 Elizabeth Taylor sold the diamond necklace containing the huge Burton-Taylor diamond for how much?
2. Which brand of watch bracelets have amongst them the Oyster, the Jubilee, and the President?
3. What was the title of the book about famous 1960's shoplifter Shirley Pitts?
4. What year did Levi's first use the lot number "501®"?
5. What year did Levi Strauss die?
6. What is patent #139,121 from the United States Patent and Trademark Office?
7. What was the name of the founder of Gucci?
8. Penhaligons famous fragrance 'Blenheim Bouquet', was created for which Duke?
9. If you bought a Bayswater or a Roxanne from Mulberry, what would you be buying?
10. Who was born Vivienne Isabel Swire in Glossop, Derbyshire?

ANSWERS

1. $5 million
2. Rolex
3. Gone Shopping
4. 1890
5. 1902
6. Levi's Jeans
7. Guccio Gucci
8. The Duke of Marlborough
9. A bag
10. Vivienne Westwood

ROUND 13
SHOPS & SHOPPING 7

QUESTIONS

1. What restaurant chain would you associate with Ray Kroc?
2. What year was eBay founded?
3. Who founded eBay?
4. True or false, people in the UK spend more money on eBay than they spend on going to the movies?
5. What is the name of the founder of Amazon?
6. How many people in the US make a living by selling on eBay?
7. What is the most expensive item sold on eBay to date?
8. At any given time, there are approximately how many million items available on eBay worldwide?
9. How many new items are added each day to eBay?
10. How many categories are there on eBay?

ANSWERS

1. McDonald's
2. 1995
3. Pierre Omidyar
4. True
5. Jeff Bezos
6. 500,000
7. A private business jet for $4.9 million
8. 44 million
9. 4 million
10. Over 50,000

ROUND 13
SHOPS & SHOPPING 8

QUESTIONS

1. Which credit card has a 13 or 16 digit number with the prefix of 4?
2. Cork St in London has a high concentration of what?
3. How much was Harrods bought for in 1985?
4. Tottenham Court Road in London is famous for buying what?
5. What kind of shop is Oddbins?
6. Christopher Wray is famous for what?
7. What are Charbonell and Walker famous for?
8. What would you associate with the Pretty Polly brand?
9. With which restaurant chain do you associate Colonel Sanders?
10. What would you find at Billingsgate market in London?

ANSWERS

1. Visa
2. Art galleries
3. £615 million
4. Electrical goods
5. Wine retailer
6. Lighting
7. Chocolate
8. Tights and stockings
9. KFC
10. Fish

ROUND 13
SHOPS & SHOPPING 9

QUESTIONS

1. What year was Harrods first floated on the London Stock Exchange under the name Harrod's Stores Limited?
2. What would you find at Smithfields market in London?
3. Which Canadian city is famed for its sprawling subterranean malls?
4. What kind of shop is Target?
5. How did Ossie Clark get the name 'Ossie'?
6. What is the name of London's oldest wine merchant?
7. Where was the first Tesco store opened in 1929?
8. The owner of which homewares store is the six richest man in the world?
9. What brand of watch broke records on 2nd December 1999 by selling at auction for $11, 002, 500?
10. Who are the World's richest cosmetics tycoons?

ANSWERS

1. 1889
2. Meat
3. Montreal
4. Drug store/phramacist
5. He was from Oswaldtwistle in Lancashire
6. Berry Brother & Rudd
7. Burnt Oak, London
8. Ikea founder, Ingvar Kamrad
9. Patek Phillipe
10. Leonard and Ronald Lauder of Estee Lauder company

ROUND 13
SHOPS & SHOPPING 10

QUESTIONS

1. Polo is a brand of which designer?
2. House of Creed specially created their Spring Flower fragrance for whom?
3. What would you be buying in Starbucks?
4. Who is the founder of Starbucks?
5. What is the largest department store in the World?
6. Who established the Habitat chain?
7. From which country does IKEA originate?
8. In 1813 Benjamin Harvey opened a linen shop in a terraced house on the corner of Knightsbridge and Sloane Street in London. What did this become?
9. Which department store's motto is Omnia Omnibus Ubique - All Things, For All People, Everywhere?
10. When was the credit card invented?

1. Ralph Lauren
2. Audrey Hepburn
3. Coffee
4. Howard Schultz
5. Macy's New York
6. Terence Conran
7. Sweden
8. Harvey Nichols
9. Harrods
10. 1950 with Diners Club's charge card

ROUND 13
SHOPS & SHOPPING 11

QUESTIONS

1. What does a greengrocer sell?
2. Which department store also has its own bank, estate agent and airline?
3. Is Macy's New York closer to the Empire State or Chrysler building?
4. The 2002 IKEA catalogue was distributed in how many different countries?
5. What Spanish footwear brand featured in an episode of Curb Your Enthusiasm?
6. Who was most associated with nickel and dime stores?
7. What year did Bank of America create the BankAmericard, (a product which eventually evolved into the Visa system)?
8. Which credit card has 15 digit number with the prefix of 34 or 37?
9. House of Creed specially created which of their fragrances for Cary Grant?
10. Which credit card has 16 digit number with the prefix of 51-55?

ANSWERS

1. Fruit and vegetables
2. Harrods
3. Empire State
4. 34
5. Camper
6. F.W. Woolworth
7. 1958
8. American Express
9. Green Irish Tweed
10. Mastercard

ROUND 13
SHOPS & SHOPPING 12

QUESTIONS

1. What is Saville Row in London famous for?
2. What is the oldest surviving booksellers in London, founded in 1797?
3. Which famous London luxury goods emporium has been in Piccadilly since 1707?
4. Which London department store has the sculpture `Winged Figure` by Barbara Hepworth, on its façade?
5. What is the world's largest second-hand bookshop?
6. How are Adidas and Puma related?
7. In 1923, who told Harper's Bazaar that "simplicity is the keynote of all true elegance"?
8. Who portrayed Coco Chanel on the Broadway stage?
9. The owner of which luxury goods store started in business selling the royal families used candles?
10. What were originally known as riveted "waist overalls"?

1. Bespoke suits
2. Hatchards, 187 Piccadilly
3. Fortnum and Mason
4. John Lewis
5. Strand on Broadway, New York
6. They were started by the rival Dassler brothers
7. Coco Chanel
8. Katharine Hepburn
9. William Fortnum of Fortnum and Mason
10. Jeans

ROUND 13
SHOPS & SHOPPING 13

QUESTIONS

1. Stella McCartney is the designer daughter of which musician?
2. What would you buy from In 'n' Out?
3. Which international health and beauty chain started in Brighton, England in 1976?
4. What year did the first Habitat store open on London's Fulham Road?
5. What does Jane Packer sell?
6. Philip Treacy is famous for making what?
7. Terry de Havilland is famous for making what?
8. Who was Raymond Clark better known as?
9. What does a furrier sell?
10. Who designed The Queen of England's wedding dress?

ANSWERS

1. Paul McCartney
2. Hamburgers
3. The Body Shop
4. 1964
5. Flowers
6. Hats
7. Shoes
8. Ossie Clark
9. Fur
10. Norman Hartnell

ROUND 13
SHOPS & SHOPPING 14

QUESTIONS

1. John Smedley is known for what?
2. What would you buy in a fromagerie?
3. Who is the shop Joseph named after?
4. What is Louis Vuitton renown for making?
5. Which American fashion designer is Donna Faske better known as?
6. Which label is miu miu closely related to?
7. Who's first runway show was the Pirate Collection shown in London in March 1981?
8. Michael Marks was co-founder of which company?
9. What year was Woolworths established in the UK?
10. Of which retailing giant is ASDA a subsidiary?

ANSWERS

1. Knitwear
2. Cheese
3. Joseph Ettedgui
4. Luggage
5. Donna Karan
6. Prada
7. Vivienne Westwood
8. Marks and Spencer
9. 1909
10. Wal*Mart

ROUND 13
SHOPS & SHOPPING 15

QUESTIONS

1. Where was the first Marks and Spencer shop?
2. What year was the 'St Michael' Marks and Spencer Trade Mark registered?
3. Over £1 in every £8 of UK retail sales is spent in which supermarket?
4. What is the largest retailer and the largest company in the world based on revenue?
5. Where did the Borders bookshop chain originate?
6. What year did the first branch of Waterstones bookshops open?
7. Who took over the Versace fashion empire when Gianni Versace was shot?
8. What year was designer Gianni Versace shot?
9. James Henry Creed founded the perfume company House of Creed in which year?
10. Which New York skyscraper is named after a retail conglomerate?

ANSWERS

1. Manchester, England
2. 1928
3. Tesco
4. Wal*Mart
5. Ann Arbor, Michigan
6. 1982
7. His sister Donnatella
8. 1997
9. 1760
10. Woolworth Building

ROUND 13
SHOPS & SHOPPING 16

QUESTIONS

1. Portobello Road is in which area of London?
2. What does Tiffany sell?
3. What colour is the famous Tiffany box?
4. What would you be shopping for in Harry Winston?
5. What is the name of the famous 3-block long stretch of boutiques and shops in Beverly Hills, CA?
6. What year was Chanel No. 5 perfume launched?
7. What did Marilyn Monroe wear to bed?
8. What is the name of Prada's little sister line?
9. What is London's Charing Cross Road famous for?
10. What London street is famed for it shirtmakers?

ANSWERS

1. Notting Hill
2. Jewellery
3. Blue
4. Diamonds
5. Rodeo Drive
6. In 1923
7. Chanel No.5
8. Miu Miu
9. Books
10. Jermyn Street

ROUND 13
SHOPS & SHOPPING 17

QUESTIONS

1. The global retail conglomerate Baugur originates from which country?
2. If you had a piece of luggage with 'LV' monogrammed on it, what would the LV stand for?
3. What country does the Muji store originate from?
4. What does KFC stand for?
5. Seditionaries' clothing is related to which fashion?
6. House of Creed specially created specially commissioned fragrances for celebrities and dignatories, who was Tabarome created for?
7. What does La Perla specialize in?
8. Statistics show the average American woman owns how many bras: two, six or eleven?
9. What year did Topshop first appear?
10. As of 2004, how many Starbucks locations were there worldwide?

ANSWERS

1. Iceland
2. Louis Vuitton
3. Japan
4. Kentucky Fried Chicken
5. Punk
6. Winston Churchill
7. Lingerie
8. Six
9. 1964
10. 8,300

ROUND 13
SHOPS & SHOPPING 18

QUESTIONS

1. What colour are the roofs of Pizza Hut restaurants?
2. What year did Louis Vuitton put out its trademark 'Monogram Canvas'?
3. House of Creed specially created their Fleurissimo fragrance for whom?
4. The first modern bra was invented in 1913 by which New York socialite?
5. Who founded the Virgin company?
6. What year did Starbucks opens its first location in Seattle's Pike Place Market?
7. How many Starbucks locations were there in 1987: 17, 30 or 3011?
8. Alannah Weston is creative director of which London department store?
9. Where is the noted department store Galleries Lafayette?
10. What American record store chain has a yellow and red logo?

ANSWERS

1. Red
2. 1896
3. Grace Kelly
4. Mary Phelps Jacob
5. Richard Branson
6. 1971
7. 17
8. Selfridges
9. Paris, France
10. Tower Records

ROUND 14

NUMBERS

dy/dt =
Cy+
π r
1/3 = √a+X

ROUND 14
NUMBERS 1

QUESTIONS

1. What year was the metric system officially adopted in France?
2. What year was saw standardisation of the inch for worldwide use?
3. In 1958, the inch was standardised worldwide as how many millimetres exactly?
4. How many cubic feet is Gross Registered Tonne (GRT)?
5. What is 78 divided by 12?
6. What is 249 multiplied by 17?
7. What is the square root of 225?
8. What date is Mother's Day in India?
9. What is 23 squared?
10. According to Forbes magazine's 2005 Rich List, Ingvar Kamprad of Sweden is the 6th richest person in the world with an estimated fortune of $23.0 billion. What store has made his fortune?

ANSWERS

1. 1799
2. 1958
3. 25.4mm
4. 100 cubic feet
5. 6.5
6. 4233
7. 15
8. May 10th
9. 529
10. IKEA

ROUND 14
NUMBERS 2

QUESTIONS

1. What system was made legal (but not mandatory) in the US by the Metric Act of 1866?
2. What percentage of the world's mail does the Japan postal service handle?
3. Half the world's population earns how much of the world's wealth?
4. More personal telephone calls are made on which day in the USA than on any other day in any other country?
5. What is 568 divided by 32?
6. What is 21 multiplied by 8?
7. What is the square root of 289?
8. What date is Mother's Day in Poland?
9. What is 2 squared ?
10. According the Sunday Times Rich List of 2005, how many billionares were there in the UK?

ANSWERS

1. The decimal system
2. 6%
3. About 5%
4. Mother's Day
5. 17.75
6. 168
7. 17
8. May 26th
9. 4
10. 40

ROUND 14
NUMBERS 3

QUESTIONS

1. In 1971, Lee Redmond of Salt Lake City broke a world record for what?
2. Whose hair clippings sold at auction in 2002 for $115,120 (£72,791)?
3. Elizabeth Ann Buttle of Wales broke the world records of years between siblings by having a gap of how many years between children?
4. Andriani Iliescu became the oldest mother on record at what age?
5. What is 68 divided by 4?
6. What is 526 multiplied by 8?
7. What is the square root of 144?
8. What date is Mother's Day in Australia?
9. What is of 13 squared?
10. According to Forbes magazine with an estimated wealth of $25.0 billion who is the third wealthiest person in the world in 2005?

ANSWERS

1. Having the world's longest nails. measuring 62.94cm each
2. Elvis Presley's
3. 41 Years 185 days
4. 66
5. 17
6. 4208
7. 12
8. The Second Sunday in May
9. 169
10. Lakshmi Mittal - UK

ROUND 14
NUMBERS 4

QUESTIONS

1. What is 12 squared?
2. According to Forbes magazine with an estimated wealth of $44.0 billion who is the second wealthiest person in the world in 2005?
3. The oldest authenticated human being was Jeanne Louise Calmet who died in 1997 at what age?
4. What is 180 divided by 10?
5. What is 112 multiplied by 21?
6. What is the square root of 49?
7. What date is Mother's Day in the UK?
8. How tall is the average American woman?
9. American Matthew McGrory has the world's biggest feet, what size are they?
10. In Japan how many days per year is the average school year?

ANSWERS

1. 144
2. Warren Buffett – USA
3. 122 years, 164 days
4. 18
5. 2352
6. 7
7. The fourth Sunday of Lent
8. 1.60m (5ft 4)
9. US 28.5
10. 243 days

ROUND 14
NUMBERS 5

QUESTIONS

1. In 1990 what word appeared in 1,583 articles in The Wall Street Journal?
2. What is 55 multiplied by 11?
3. What is 6842 divided by 22?
4. What is the square root of 1764?
5. What date is Remembrance Day?
6. What date is Boxing Day?
7. What is the world's biggest industry, affecting 240 million jobs?
8. What is this a formula for finding: (a _ b)2 = a2 _ 2ab + b2 ?
9. Where on the Sunday Times Rich List does The Queen appear?
10. What is 5 squared?

ANSWERS

1. Recession
2. 605
3. 311
4. 42
5. November 11th
6. December 26th
7. Tourism.
8. The square root of a number
9. Fifteenth
10. 25

ROUND 14
NUMBERS 6

QUESTIONS

1. In the US, which month is murder committed least frequently?
2. The world average consumption of what food is 230 per capita?.
3. In the US, approximately how many million turkeys are sold for the Thanksgiving celebrations?
4. What percentage of the world's population is under 25 years of age?
5. What is 36 divided by 12?
6. What is 86 multiplied by 3?
7. What is the square root of 529?
8. What date is Mother's Day in Costa Rica?
9. What is 25 squared ?
10. How many self-made millionaires appeared in the Sunday Times Rich List of 2005?

ANSWERS

1. February
2. Egg
3. About 280 million
4. 50%
5. 3
6. 258
7. 23
8. August 15th
9. 625

751

ROUND 14
NUMBERS 7

QUESTIONS

1. Roy C Sullivan of Virginia has been struck by lightning how many times?
2. Who holds the world record for the fastest six digit square root calculation without a calculator?
3. Who is the world's youngest millionairess, with a wealth exceeding $1million (equivalent to $8, 932,472 today) dollars before she was 10 in 1932?
4. What year was the metric system introduced into Europe?
5. What is 525 divided by 5?
6. What is 653 multiplied by 2?
7. What is the square root of 81?
8. What date is Mother's Day in Japan?
9. What is 17 squared?
10. According to Forbes magazine with an estimated wealth of $23.8 billion who is the fourth wealthiest person in the world in 2005?

ANSWERS

1. 7
2. M Hari Prasad of Bangalore, India. He did it in 1min 38 secs
3. Shirley Temple
4. In 1202
5. 105
6. 1306
7. 9
8. The Second Sunday in May
9. 289
10. Carlos Slim Helú - Mexico

ROUND 14

NUMBERS 8

QUESTIONS

1. According to Forbes magazine, who is the wealthiest person in the world in 2005?
2. In a 1995 Russian census, men and women had the biggest gap in gender life expectancy by how many years?
3. As of January 17 2005 Emiliano Mercado Del Toro of Puerto Rica Oldest authenticated living man at what age?
4. As of May 29th 2004, Hendrikje Van Andel-Shipper was the oldest woman in the world at how old?
5. What date is Groundhog Day in United States and Canada?
6. What is 225 divided by 15?
7. What is 52 multiplied by 52?
8. What is the square root of 9?
9. What date is Mother's Day in the US?
10. What is 8 squared?

ANSWERS

1. Bill Gates
2. 13.43 years
3. 113 years, 149 days
4. 113 years, 335 days
5. February 2
6. 15
7. 2704
8. 3
9. The Second Sunday in May
10. 64

ROUND 14
NUMBERS 9

QUESTIONS

1. In Sweden, how many days per year is the average school year?
2. In the developed countries, the proportion of adults married has declined from 72% in 1970 to what percentage in 1996?
3. What is 255665 divided by 2?
4. What is 45 multiplied by 20?
5. What is the square root of 784?
6. What date is Fathers' Day in the US?
7. What is 14 squared?
8. What is the name of annual list of the 1,000 richest people in the UK?
9. What date is Earth Day?
10. How many millimetres in one metre?

ANSWERS

1. 170 days
2. 60%
3. 127832.5
4. 900
5. 28
6. The third Sunday in June
7. 196
8. The Sunday Times Rich List
9. April 22
10. 1000

ROUND 14
NUMBERS 10

QUESTIONS

1. On average in the West how frequently do people move house?
2. What percentage of the world's mail does the US Post Office handle?
3. How many days per year is the world's average school year?
4. In the US, how many days per year is the average school year?
5. What is 9500 divided by 50?
6. What is 9478 multiplied by 45?
7. What is the square root of 625?
8. What year did Lyndon Johnson make Father's Day a holiday in the US?
9. What is 31 squared?
10. How many of the 1000 people listed in the Sunday Times Rich List of 2005 inherited their wealth?

ANSWERS

1. Every 7 years
2. 43%
3. 200 days
4. 180 days
5. 190
6. 426510
7. 25
8. 1966
9. 961
10. 249

ROUND 14
NUMBERS 11

QUESTIONS

1. What would a million dollars' worth of $100 bills weigh?
2. What date is April Fool's Day?
3. In the developed countries what is the chance of a second marriage ending in divorce as a percentage?
4. What is 88 divided by 8?
5. What is 325 multiplied by 512?
6. What is the square root of 1024?
7. What date is Fathers' Day in Bulgaria?
8. What is 43 squared?
9. According the Sunday Times Rich List of 2005, who is the richest woman in the UK?
10. If you stack one million US$1 bills, what would it weigh?

ANSWERS

1. Only 10 kg (22 lb).
2. April 1st
3. Between 60% and 77%
4. 10
5. 166400
6. 32
7. June 20th
8. 1849
9. J.K.Rowling
10. Exactly 1 ton

ROUND 14
NUMBERS 12

QUESTIONS

1. How many women were in the Sunday Times Rich List of 2005 (out of 1000 entries)?
2. What ratio of people in the world live on an island?
3. The opposite sides of a dice cube always add up to how many?
4. In the US, which month is murder committed most frequently?
5. What date is World Aids day?
6. What is 568 divided by 200?
7. What is 6542 multiplied by 2?
8. What is the square root of 361?
9. What date is Mother's Day in Russia?
10. What is 6 squared?

ANSWERS

1. 78
2. One in ten
3. 7
4. August
5. December 1st
6. 2.84
7. 13084
8. 19
9. November 28th
10. 36

ROUND 14
NUMBERS 13

QUESTIONS

1. What date is Mother's Day in Mexico?
2. What is 20 squared?
3. According to Forbes magazine, with an estimated wealth of $23.7 billion who is the fifth wealthiest person in the world in 2005?
4. Italian mathematician Leonardo of Pisa is also known as whom?
5. What is 45 divided by 12?
6. What is 78 multiplied by 68?
7. What is the square root of 169?
8. What measuring unit comes from the Latin "mille passus", based on the Roman Legion's 1,000 paces?
9. "Decimal" is derived from the Latin word for what number?
10. What word, adopted in 1793 by the French Academy of Science, derived from the Greek word "metron", meaning "a measure"?

ANSWERS

1. May 10th
2. 400
3. Alwaleed Bin Talal Alsaud - Saudi Arabia
4. Fibonacci
5. 3.75
6. 5304
7. 13
8. The Mile
9. Ten
10. The word „metre"

ROUND 14

NUMBERS 14

QUESTIONS

1. The chance of being born on leap day is about 1 in how many?
2. How many people in the world have their birthday on leap day?
3. The odds of being struck by what are about 600,000 to one?
4. Approximately what percentage of food in developed countries is wasted each year by being thrown away?
5. What is 7000 divided by 100?
6. What is 31 multiplied by 864?
7. What is the square root of 484?
8. What date is Mother's Day in Indonesia?
9. What is 21 squared?
10. How many ounces are in a pound?

ANSWERS

1. 1461
2. 4.1 million
3. Lightning
4. About 27%
5. 70
6. 26784
7. 22
8. December 22nd
9. 441
10. 16

ROUND 14
NUMBERS 15

QUESTIONS

1. How much is annual global spending on education (in US $)?
2. What is the average age of Forbes's 400 wealthiest individuals?
3. What is 888 divided by 8?
4. What is 10 multiplied by 20?
5. What is the square root of 1225?
6. What date is VE day?
7. What is 49 squared?
8. According the Sunday Times Rich List of 2005, who is the second richest woman in the UK?
9. What date is May Day?
10. Where does the term "Blue Chip" comes from?

ANSWERS

1. $80 billion
2. 63
3. 111
4. 200
5. 35
6. May 8th
7. 2401
8. The Queen
9. May 1st
10. The colour of the poker chip with the highest value, blue

ROUND 14

NUMBERS 16

QUESTIONS

1. In 1900, what was the price of gold (in US$)?
2. in 1930 the price of gold was $600 per ounce, what is the current price?
3. What is 6882 divided by 444?
4. What is 65 multiplied by 65?
5. What is the square root of 1444?
6. What date is VJ day?
7. What is 19 squared?
8. Which UK novelist is richer than the Queen?
9. Who are the two richest women in the world?
10. Tobacco is an industry worth how much?

ANSWERS

1. Less than $40 per ounce
2. About $430 per ounce
3. 15.5
4. 4225
5. 38
6. August 15th
7. 361
8. J.K.Rowling
9. Alice and Helen Walton of Wal*Mart fame: $18 billion each
10. $200 billion

ROUND 14
NUMBERS 17

QUESTIONS

1. What percentage of his wealth did Elton John give to charity in 2005?
2. In the developed countries what is the chance of a first marriage ending in divorce as a percentage?
3. According to the US Census Bureau, what percentage of US children live in poverty?
4. What would one million dollars' worth of once-cent coins (100 million coins) weigh?
5. In 1998, US states spent $30 billion in funds on what services?
6. What is 78 divided by 4?
7. What is 98 multiplied by 40?
8. What is the square root of 841?
9. What date is Fathers' Day in the UK?
10. What is 45 squared?

ANSWERS

1. 12%
2. Between 50% and 67%
3. 19%
4. 246 tons
5. Correctional
6. 19.5
7. 3920
8. 29
9. The third Sunday in June
10. 2025

ROUND 14
NUMBERS 18

QUESTIONS

1. The word millionaire was first used by Benjamin Disraeli in which 1826 novel?
2. According to Forbes' 19th annual list of the richest people published in 2005 there are how many US-dollar billionaires in the world?
3. Merrill Lynch and Capgemini compile which financial annual report?
4. What is 33 divided by 3?
5. What is 897 multiplied by 4?
6. What is the square root of 961?
7. What date is Fathers' Day in Spain?
8. What is 37 squared?
9. How many aristocrats appeared on the 2005 Sunday Times Rich List?
10. According to the US Weather Service, their one day forecasts are accurate more than what percentage of the time?

ANSWERS

1. Vivian Grey
2. 691.
3. The World Wealth Report
4. 11
5. 3588
6. 31
7. March 19th
8. 1369
9. 136
10. 75%

ROUND 15

TRAVEL &

GEOGRAPHY

ROUND 15
TRAVEL & GEOGRAPHY 1

QUESTIONS

1. What percentage of Iceland is volcanically active?
2. Record-breaking attempts to cross the Atlantic started and finished where?
3. What is the National airline of Ireland?
4. Name the capital of Slovenia?
5. What is Nessie?
6. Which language has the most native speakers?
7. What year did Hurricane Mitch strike Honduras and Nicaragua?
8. Which country is the sixth largest oil supplier to the US?
9. How many islands in the British Isles?
10. What is the largest lake in North America?

ANSWERS

1. 30%
2. Bishop Rock, The Scilly Isles
3. Aer Lingus
4. Ljubljana
5. The loch ness monster
6. Mandarin
7. 1998
8. Iraq
9. 1,040
10. Lake Superior

ROUND 15
TRAVEL & GEOGRAPHY 2

QUESTIONS

1. What year did Captain Cook set sail to circumnavigate the globe?
2. Which country's stamps are the only ones in the world not to bear the name of the country of origin?
3. What is the national airline of Lebanon?
4. What is the capital of Denmark?
5. What is the world's third most populated country?
6. Which is the smallest independent island country?
7. What year did Krakatoa erupt?
8. Where was Christopher Columbus originally from?
9. In 1887, the Yellow River broke its banks in China. How many people died?
10. What year did Mont Pelée erupt in the Caribbean killing 40,000 people?

1. 1768
2. United Kingdom
3. Middle East Airlines
4. Copenhagen
5. USA
6. The Pacific island of Nauru
7. 1883
8. Italy
9. 1 million
10. 1902

ROUND 15
TRAVEL & GEOGRAPHY 3

QUESTIONS

1. What year did the Spain and Portugal sign the Treaty of Tordesillas?
2. Where is the world's highest waterfall?
3. What country would you find the towns of Plovdiv and Burgas?
4. What is the capital of Malta?
5. What is the largest volcano?
6. What magnitude was the San Francisco earthquake of 1906?
7. What year was Christopher Columbus born?
8. What is the National airline of the Bahamas?
9. What is the smallest island in the world?
10. Who was the first explorer to map out the North American coast

ANSWERS

1. 1494
2. Angel Falls, Venezuela (979 meters).
3. Bulgaria
4. Valletta
5. The Mauna Loa volcano in Hawaii
6. 8.3
7. 1451
8. Bahamasair
9. Bishop Rock
10. Cabot

ROUND 15
TRAVEL & GEOGRAPHY 4

QUESTIONS

1. What is the currency of Laos?
2. What country would you find the towns of Quebec and Winninpeg?
3. What is the capital of Morocco?
4. What year was Captain James Cook appointed Naval Commander?
5. What year did "The Great Hurricane" hit the Caribbean?
6. How many weeks after setting sail did Columbus sight San Salvador?
7. Which discoverer of the Americas called himself "Al Almirante"?
8. Born in 1480, Diego Colón was the son of which explorer?
9. Where did Columbus think he had reached on his discovery of the Americas?
10. What is the true circumference of the earth at the equator in kilometers?

ANSWERS

1. Kip
2. Canada
3. Rabat
4. 1771
5. 1780
6. 10 weeks
7. Christopher Columbus
8. Christopher Columbus
9. Asia
10. 40,000

ROUND 15
TRAVEL & GEOGRAPHY 5

QUESTIONS

1. In what country would you find the towns of Zeebrugge and Ghent?
2. What water temperature is necessary for hurricanes to form?
3. Which is the world's most tornado-prone country?
4. What is the national airline of Finland?
5. What is the capital of Japan?
6. What percentage of the world's population lives under the threat of volcanoes?
7. How many years before Columbus did the Vikings arrive in America?
8. What year did King Henry VII grant John Cabot a charter to explore?
9. What is the currency of Switzerland?
10. London experienced an earthquake with a magnitude of 4 in what year?

ANSWERS

1. Belgium
2. 26.5C (79.7F)
3. UK because of its large coastline to surface area ratio
4. Finnair
5. Tokyo
6. 10%
7. 500 years
8. 1497
9. Swiss Franc
10. 1938

ROUND 15
TRAVEL & GEOGRAPHY 6

QUESTIONS

1. In which ocean would you find Tristan da Cunha island?
2. What year did Typhoon Toraji slam into central Taiwan and China?
3. What is the capital of Indonesia?
4. Which country has the biggest population?
5. What is the world's second most populated country?
6. The 2004 Indian Ocean tsunami killed over 200,000 people on which date?
7. How many of the world's volcanoes are active?
8. What is the currency of Pakistan?
9. What country would you find the towns of Cordoba and Mendoza?
10. Tsunamis travel how fast?

ANSWERS

1. South Atlantic
2. 2001
3. Jakarta
4. China
5. India
6. December 26th
7. 900
8. Pakistan Rupee
9. Argentina
10. 500 km/h (311 mph)

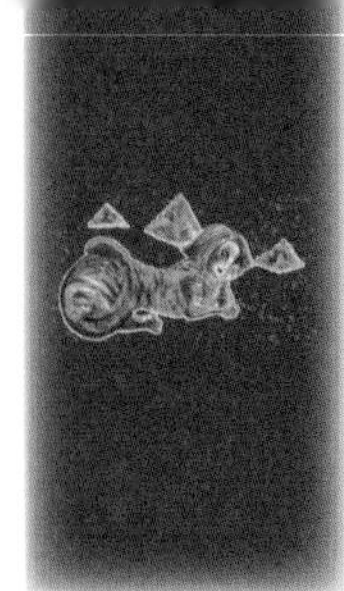

ROUND 15
TRAVEL & GEOGRAPHY 7

QUESTIONS

1. Francis Drake returned from his global navigation in which year?
2. What is the currency of Mexico?
3. What location recorded the world's hottest temperature?
4. What is the capital of Turkey?
5. Which is the world's largest ocean?
6. What is the largest lake in the world?
7. How much of the Earth's land surface is desert?
8. What is the highest, driest, and coldest continent on Earth?
9. The sandspit at the mouth of England's River Humber is known as what?
10. What island lies between England, Scotland, and Ireland?

ANSWERS

1. 1580
2. Mexican Peso
3. El Azizia in Libya (57.8 C/136F)
4. Ankara
5. Pacific (165 million square km)
6. Caspian Sea
7. 30%
8. Antarctica
9. Spurn Head
10. Isle of Man

ROUND 15
TRAVEL & GEOGRAPHY 8

QUESTIONS

1. Which is the only country where Latin is the official language?
2. What is the capital of Bangladesh?
3. Which is the only country in the world where all the citizens speak one language?
4. Which set of continents were named after Amerigo Vespucci in 1507?
5. Who was the first man to sail around the world alone?
6. Which mythical creature is protected by the 1912 Protection of Animals Acts of Scotland?
7. What is the National airline of Panama?
8. Which shipping company introduced the first round-the-world cruise?
9. What is the world population expected to be in 40 years?
10. Half the population of the World are under what age?

ANSWERS

1. The Vatican
2. Dhaka
3. Somalia
4. The Americas
5. Joshua Slocum
6. The Loch Ness Monster
7. Copa
8. Cunard
9. 12 billion
10. 25

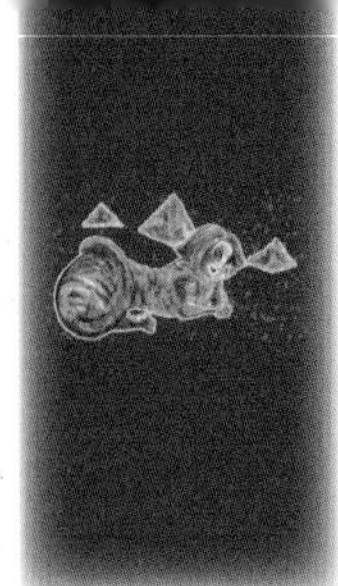

ROUND 15
TRAVEL & GEOGRAPHY 9

QUESTIONS

1. What is the currency of Brazil?
2. What is the national airline of Latvia?
3. What is the capital of El Salvador?
4. How long had Mt St Helen been dormant before exploding in 1980?
5. What year did Mount Tambora in Indonesia erupt, resulting in the death of 10,000 people?
6. What year did Captain Cook reach Tahiti?
7. Between 1876 – 79 what deadly natural disaster struck China?
8. What is the national airline of France?
9. The world single most devastating tornado killed 695 Americans. What year did it strike?
10. Britain experienced a 6.1 magnitude earthquake in what year?

ANSWERS

1. Cruzado
2. Air Baltic
3. San Salvador
4. 1815
5. 1769
6. 9 million people?
7. A drought
8. Air France
9. 1925
10. 1931

ROUND 15
TRAVEL & GEOGRAPHY 10

QUESTIONS

1. What is the national airline of Russia?
2. What is the capital of Afghanistan?
3. How many ships set sail on Chistopher Columbus's second voyage?
4. What year did the British government set out the parameters for classifying an island?
5. What is the remotest uninhabited island?
6. Which country consists of 13,667 islands – 6,000 of which are inhabited?
7. How many islands does Finland claim in its waters?
8. Which South American nation was unfortunate enough to witness the world's most powerful earthquake in 1960?
9. Which is the remotest inhabited island in the world?
10. The word "volcano" dervives from which Roman god?

ANSWERS

1. Aeroflot
2. Kabul
3. Seventeen
4. 1861
5. Bouvet Island in the South Atlantic
6. Indonesia
7. 180,000
8. Chile
9. Tristan da Cunha
10. Vulcan

ROUND 15
TRAVEL & GEOGRAPHY 11

QUESTIONS

1. What is the national airline of Luxembourg?
2. Which ancient Egyptian burial monuments built during the Old and Middle Kingdom periods have associations with royal solar and stellar cults?
3. Which island lies at the most south-westerly part of the United Kingdom?
4. The Great Pyramid presides over which plateau on the outskirts of Cairo?
5. Which is the largest lake in England?
6. What year was the first propeller driven Atlantic crossing?
7. What is the national airline of Greece?
8. Which is the deepest lake in England?
9. How long did it take to complete the first circumnavigation of earth by air?
10. What year did Captain Cook reach New Zealand?

ANSWERS

1. LuxAir
2. The Pyramids
3. Bishop Rock
4. Giza
5. Windermere
6. 1845
7. Olympic Airways
8. Wastwater
9. 175 days
10. 1769

ROUND 15
TRAVEL & GEOGRAPHY 12

QUESTIONS

1. What is the national airline of Russia?
2. What is the capital of Afghanistan?
3. How many ships set sail on Chistopher Columbus's second voyage?
4. What year did the British government set out the parameters for classifying an island?
5. What is the remotest uninhabited island?
6. Which country consists of 13,667 islands – 6,000 of which are inhabited?
7. How many islands does Finland claim in its waters?
8. Which South American nation was unfortunate enough to witness the world's most powerful earthquake in 1960?
9. Which is the remotest inhabited island in the world? .
10. The word "volcano" dervives from which Roman god?

ANSWERS

1. Maya Island Air
2. Port-au-Prince
3. Six
4. 25,000 miles
5. 1981
6. 1995
7. 1998
8. British Airways
9. Euro
10. Algeria

ROUND 15
TRAVEL & GEOGRAPHY 13

QUESTIONS

1. Of the 6 billion people in the world what percentage of them live on an island?
2. Which is the only island nation connected to a continent?
3. Roughly how many different languages are spoken in the world today?
4. What is the national airline of Poland?
5. Which language is the world's most widely spoken?
6. What is the National airline of Germany?
7. What is the capital of Algeria?
8. What is the world's newest language?
9. How many ethnic groups exist in China?
10. The US Census Bureau reported that the 6 billionth person was born at 1.24am on Sunday 18 July in which year?

ANSWERS

1. 10%
2. Britain (through the Chunnel).
3. More than 2,700
4. LOT Polish Airlines
5. English
6. Lufthansa
7. Algiers
8. Afrikaans
9. 55
10. 1999

ROUND 15
TRAVEL & GEOGRAPHY 14

QUESTIONS

1. What is the national airline of Jordan?
2. What's the capital of Rwanda?
3. What year was the first steam assisted Atlantic crossing?
4. The world's first underground passenger railway opened in 1863 in which city?
5. What is the world's smallest ocean?
6. What is the population of Finland?
7. How many different languages are spoken in Indonesia?
8. Where is the largest island in the world?
9. What year was Greenland granted home rule within the Danish Commonwealth?
10. What is the longest river in the Untied States?

ANSWERS

1. Royal Jordanian Airlines
2. Kigali
3. 1819
4. London
5. The Arctic Ocean
6. Five million
7. 365
8. Greenland
9. 1979
10. Mississippi

ROUND 15
TRAVEL & GEOGRAPHY 15

QUESTIONS

1. In what country would you find the towns of Paphos and Limassol?
2. What country would you find the towns of Asmara and Dire Diwa?
3. What is the capital of New Zealand?
4. What year did Columbus set out on his third voyage of discovery ?
5. Who was the second man to captain a circumnavigation of the globe?
6. Roughly how many different languages are spoken in London?
7. What is the currency of Hungary?
8. What year was Francis Drake born?
9. What year did Francis Drake set sail to circumnavigate the globe?
10. In September 1578, where did five of Francis Drake's ships turn back?

ANSWERS

1. Cyprus
2. Ethiopia
3. Wellington
4. 1498
5. Francis Drake
6. 700
7. Forint
8. 1540
9. 1577
10. At the Strait of Magellan

ROUND 15
TRAVEL & GEOGRAPHY 16

QUESTIONS

1. What is the capital of Papua New Guinea?
2. What was the name of Captain Cook's circumnavigating ship?
3. Who was the first woman to sail solo around the world in 1979?
4. What is the national airline of Australia?
5. What year did Columbus set sail for his second voyage?
6. How far below sea level is the Dead Sea?
7. What country would you find the towns of Thessaloniki and Patras?
8. Which is the most earthquake-prone state in the United States?
9. Which country has the world's driest location?
10. What year was the largest ever earthquake?

ANSWERS

1. Port Moresby
2. Endeavour
3. Dame Naomi James.
4. Qantas
5. 1493
6. 400m
7. Greece
8. Alaska
9. Chile (Arica with only 0.76 millimeters rainfall per year)
10. 1960

ROUND 15
TRAVEL & GEOGRAPHY 17

QUESTIONS

1. What is the national airline of Trinidad and Tobago
2. What is the capital of Fiji?
3. The Columbian Exchange refers to what?
4. San Francisco witnessed its most devastating earthquake in which year?
5. What is the population of the world's most remote island in the world, Tristan da Cunha?
6. A devastating 8.3 earthquake hit northeast China killing 240,000 people in which year?
7. What year did hurricane David hit the Caribbean and Eastern U.S?
8. What year did Mount St Helen explode?
9. What is the National airline of Morocco?
10. What was the name of the ship Francis Drake sailed in to circumnavigate the globe?

ANSWERS

1. BWIA
2. Suva on Viti Levu
3. The exchange of agricultural goods and communicable diseases between the Eastern and Western Hemispheres that occurred after 1492
4. 1906
5. 242
6. 1976
7. 1979
8. 1980
9. Royal Air Maroc
10. The Golden Hind

ROUND 15
TRAVEL & GEOGRAPHY 18

QUESTIONS

1. What is the currency of Sweden?
2. What country would you find the towns of Chiclayo and Arequipa?
3. What is the capital of Portugal?
4. What mountain range divides France and Spain?
5. What is Britain's longest river?
6. Which of Magellan's five ships to set out to first circumnavigate the globe was burned?
7. In September 1519 who set sail with 280 men on 5 ships to circumnavigate the globe?
8. What year did Christopher Columbus reach the Americas?
9. What location recorded the world's coldest temperature?
10. What is the highest mountain?

ANSWERS

1. Krona
2. Peru
3. Lisbon
4. Pyrenees
5. Servern
6. The Conception
7. The Tynwald on the Isle of Man
8. 1492
9. Vostok, Antarctica (-89 C on July 21. 1983)
10. Mount Everest

ROUND 16

BOOKS &

ITERATURE

ROUND 16
BOOKS & LITERATURE 1

QUESTIONS

1. Alice Pleasance Liddell was the inspiration for which book?
2. Who wrote 'Tom Sawyer'?
3. Who wrote 'Call of the Wild'?
4. Which novelist and science fiction writer wrote 'The Time Machine'?
5. Who won the Booker Prize in1981?
6. Which multi-millionare novelist was unemployed, whilst writing her first book?
7. What does the H G in H G Wells stand for?
8. Who's autobiographical book of "alcoholic memoirs," 'John Barleycorn', was published in 1913?
9. Who wrote 'The Wind in the Willows'?
10. Who was Ted Hughes famously married to?

ANSWERS

1. 'Alice's Adventures in Wonder-land'
2. Mark Twain
3. Jack London
4. H G Wells
5. Salman Rushdie for 'Midnight's Children'
6. J K Rowling of Harry Potter fame
7. Herbert George
8. Jack London
9. Kenneth Grahame
10. Sylvia Plath

ROUND 16
BOOKS & LITERATURE 2

QUESTIONS

1. Which 1857 novel tells the story of a doctor's wife who commits suicide after a series of unhappy love affairs?
2. What is classed as Goethe's masterpiece?
3. Which imaginary county are Thomas Hardy's novels set?
4. Who has his heart buried at Stinsford and his ashes were interred in Westminster Abbey?
5. Where do the police catch up with Tess and Angel in Tess of the d'Urbervilles?
6. Who wrote The Iliad?
7. Who wrote the supernatural tale The Turn of the Screw?
8. Lady Chatterley's Lover was written in which year?
9. Which 1928 book was banned as obscene in the UK until 1960?
10. What was the name of Proust's mammoth autobiographical series of novels?

ANSWERS

1. Madame Bovary
2. Faust, 1808
3. Wessex
4. Thomas Hardy
5. Stonehenge
6. Homer
7. Henry James
8. 1928
9. Lady Chatterley's Lover
10. Remembrance of Things Past

ROUND 16
BOOKS & LITERATURE 3

QUESTIONS

1. In 1782, which British mystical poet and artist married a poor illiterate girl named Catherine Boucher?
2. What is the surname of sister novelists charlotte, Emily and Anne?
3. Who wrote the poem 'To A Mouse'?
4. What was Dickens' first novel?
5. In which book does Sancho Panza appear?
6. Who wrote the Canterbury Tales?
7. What is Dante's greatest work?
8. What year was Robinson Crusoe published?
9. Who wrote Don Juan?
10. How long did Robinson Crusoe spend on the island?

ANSWERS

1. William Blake
2. Bronte
3. Robert Burns
4. The Pickwick Papers.
5. Don Quixote
6. Geoffrey Chaucer
7. The Divine Comedy
8. 1719
9. Byron
10. 28 years

ROUND 16
BOOKS & LITERATURE 4

QUESTIONS

1. What year was Oliver Twist published?
2. Who completed a novel every two weeks, publishing 723 novels?
3. What is the world's best selling book?
4. Which 1996 book chronicled the life of, a thirty something single woman living in London, trying to make sense of life and love in the 1990s?
5. Ian Fleming's character debuted in the novel "Casino Royale" in 1952?
6. Who wrote the first English dictionary in 1755?
7. Which Jonathan Swift book published in 1726, was intended as a satire on the ferociousness of human nature. Today it is enjoyed as a children's story?
8. When was the first Oxford English Dictionary published?
9. Which sexy text was written by Vatsyayana sometime between the 1st to 6th centuries A.D?
10. Which literary family lived at Haworth Rectory in Yorkshire?

ANSWERS

1. 1838
2. Barbara Cartland
3. The Bible
4. Bridget Jones's Diary
5. James Bond
6. Samuel Johnson
7. 'Gulliver's Travels'
8. 1884
9. The Karma Sutra
10. The Brontes

ROUND 16
BOOKS & LITERATURE 5

QUESTIONS

1. What was Agatha Christie's first novel?
2. Who was the first poet to win a Pulitzer Prize posthumously for The Collected Poems?
3. In 1984 who declined the role of Poet Laureate?
4. Which epic Tolstoy novel deals with the Napleonic Wars?
5. Who published a collection of poems entitled Birthday Letters?
6. In 1847 who wrote Agnes Grey?
7. What year was the Booker Prize for Fiction established?
8. Who is the only person to have been nominated six times for The Booker Prize?
9. Who won the first Booker Prize?
10. Who wrote 'Mein Kampf/My Struggle'?

ANSWERS

1. 'The Mysterious Affair at Styles' 1920
2. Sylvia Plath
3. Philip Larkin
4. War and Peace
5. Ted Hughes
6. Anne Bronte
7. 1968
8. Iris Murdoch
9. Percy Howard Newby for 'Something to Answer For'
10. Adolf Hitler

ROUND 16
BOOKS & LITERATURE 6

QUESTIONS

1. What book won the Pulitzer Prize for fiction in 2003?
2. The inscription on who's tomb reads: “He was a sympathiser to the poor, the suffering, and the oppressed; and by his death, one of England's greatest writers is lost to the world.”?
3. Which Russian novelist was sent to prison for four years accused of being a social revolutionary?
4. Which book opens with the line “Last night I dreamt I went to Manderley again”?
5. Who wrote and illustrated Jerusalem 1804-1820?
6. Who wrote Crime and Punishment in 1866?
7. Novelist Mary Ann Evans is better known as who?
8. Which novel would you find Tom and Maggie Tulliver?
9. Which author lies buried in Le Père Lachaise Cemetery, Paris beneath a Rodin sculpture?
10. Which 1980s musical used T S Eliots' collection Old Possum's Book of Practical Cats?

ANSWERS

1. 'Middlesex' by Jeffrey Eugenides
2. Charles Dickens
3. Dostoevsky
4. Rebecca
5. William Blake
6. Dostoevsky
7. George Eliot
8. The Mill on the Floss
9. Balzac
10. Cats

ROUND 16
BOOKS & LITERATURE 7

QUESTIONS

1. Who Created Sherlock Holmes?
2. The 'Black Dahlia' was the nickname for which woman?
3. Which was Jane Austen's first book?
4. At age twelve which author worked a 10 hour day in a boot-blacking factory?
5. Which novel would you find Mr Darcy?
6. Which books lead character is 20 year old Elizabeth Bennet?
7. Romance writer Mary Westmacott was better known as who?
8. Which author's Human Comedy (La Comédie humaine) spanned more than 90 novels and short stories?
9. Who wrote The Black Dahlia?
10. Who wrote the 1857 volume of poems, 'Les fleurs du mal'?

ANSWERS

1. Arthur Conan Doyle
2. Elizabeth Short
3. Northanger Abbey
4. Charles Dickens
5. Pride and Predjudice
6. Pride and Predjudice
7. Agatha Christie
8. France Honoré de Balzac
9. James Ellroy
10. Charles Pierre Baudelaire

ROUND 16
BOOKS & LITERATURE 8

QUESTIONS

1. What year was William Shakespeare born?
2. At the request of which queen is Shakespeare said to have written 'The Merry Wives of Windsor'?
3. What book won the Pulitzer Prize for fiction in 1999?
4. Which English poet did Mary Wollstonecraft Godwin marry?
5. The word boredom first appeared in print in which Dickens novel?
6. What famous novel did Mary Wollstonecraft Godwin write under her married name? Frankenstein.
7. Jonathan Swift is most famous for which satire novel?
8. Which area of England is known as Wordsworth country?
9. Who wrote Dictionary of Trite Ideas?
10. What poet would be expected to compose poems for state occasions and other government events?

ANSWERS

1. 1564
2. Elizabeth I
3. 'The Hours' by Michael Cunningham
4. Shelley
5. Bleak House
6. She became Mary Shelley in 1816
7. Gulliver's Travels
8. The Lake District
9. Gustave Flaubert
10. The Poet Laureate

ROUND 16
BOOKS & LITERATURE 9

QUESTIONS

1. Humbert Humbert is a character in which controversial book?
2. In John Fowles' 1963 book 'The Collector',
what does Frederick Clegg collect?
3. Who won the Booker Prize in 1990?
4. Who wrote 'For Whom the Bell Tolls'?
5. Who wrote 'Charlie and the Chocolate Factory'?
6. In the 1965 film adaptation of John Fowles book
'The' Collector, who plays Frederick Clegg?
7. Who wrote 'Gone with the Wind'?
8. Which book won the Pulitzer Prize on May 3, 1937?
9. Which John Steinbeck novella has George
and Lennie as its main characters?
10. Who was awarded the Nobel Prize for literature in 1962?

ANSWERS

1. Lolita' by Vladimir Nabokov
2. 'Butterflies
3. A.S. Byatt for 'Possession'
4. Ernest Hemingway
5. Roald Dahl
6. Terence Stamp
7. Margaret Mitchell
8. 'Gone with the Wind'
9. 'Of Mice and Men'
10. John Steinbeck

ROUND 16
BOOKS & LITERATURE 10

QUESTIONS

1. In Daphne Du Mauriers' book Rebecca what is the name of the husband?
2. Who was Lady Chatterley's lover?
3. Who is the all time best selling author in France?
4. How many Bond novels did Ian Fleming write?
5. What is Miss Marple's first name?
6. What animal is Boxer in George Orwell's Animal Farm?
7. Who wrote The Day of the Jackal?
8. Who created female sleuth Cordelia Gray?
9. What was Arthur Conan Doyles day job?
10. Who is the domineering housekeeper in the book Rebecca?

ANSWERS

1. Maximilian de Winter
2. Oliver Mellors
3. Agatha Christie
4. Twelve
5. Jane
6. A horse
7. Frederick Forsythe
8. P D James
9. Doctor
10. Mrs. Danvers

ROUND 16
BOOKS & LITERATURE 11

QUESTIONS

1. Who wrote My Dark Places?
2. Who wrote Moby Dick?
3. Who wrote Dracula?
4. Who wrote The Mill on the Floss?
5. What was John Dawkins' nickname in Oliver Twist?
6. Which author created the detective Philip Marlowe?
7. Which author created Dr Kay Scarpetta?
8. Which Dickens novel was published in 1854?
9. Who wrote 2004 book The Lovely Bones?
10. Who wrote The Time Machine?

ANSWERS

1. James Ellroy
2. Herman Melville
3. Bram Stoker
4. George Eliot
5. The Artful Dodger
6. Raymond Chandler
7. Patricia Cornwell
8. Hard Times
9. Alice Sebold
10. H G Wells

ROUND 16
BOOKS & LITERATURE 12

QUESTIONS

1. Which John Steinbeck book starred James Dean in the film version?
2. The movie adaptation of which book starred Renée Zellweger as the famous 90's diarist?
3. Which was the first book in the Harry Potter series?
4. Who attends the Hogwarts School of Witchcraft and Wizardry?
5. Who's autobiography was titled 'The Moon's a Balloon'?
6. Which 1996 political book's success was in part fueled by speculation over the identity of the author?
7. In which Dickens novel is Sissy Jupe adopted by Thomas Gradgrind?
8. In which book of the Old Testament are the ten commandments written?
9. What is Quasimodo also know as?
10. Which play is generally agreed to be Shakespeare's last?

ANSWERS

1. 'East of Eden'
2. Bridget Jones's Diary
3. 'Harry Potter and the Philosopher's Stone' (1997)
4. Harry Potter
5. David Niven
6. 'Primary Colors' by Anonymous
7. 'Hard Times'
8. Exodus
9. The Hunchback of Notre Dame
10. The Tempest

ROUND 16
BOOKS & LITERATURE 13

QUESTIONS

1. Which book published in 1913 depicts the outward and inward life of an alcoholic and is recommended by Alcoholics Anonymous?
2. What year did The Cat in the Hat first appear?
3. What was the title of Sylvia Plath's only novel?
4. Who wrote the play An Inspector Calls?
5. In which book does Don Vito Corleone appear?
6. Which Dickens novel takes place in the fictional Coketown?
7. In 'Alice's Adventures in Wonderland' who gives the famous riddle without an answer: "Why is a raven like a writing desk?"?
8. September 1988 saw the publication of which controversial book by Salman Rushdie?
9. Which Jane Austen book was originally called Susan?
10. 'All the President's Men' was an account of what?

ANSWERS

1. 'John Barleycorn' by Jack London
2. 1957
3. The Bell Jar
4. J B Priestley
5. The Godfather
6. Hard Times
7. The Mad Hatter
8. 'The Satanic Verses'
9. Northanger Abbey
10. The Watergate Scandal

ROUND 16
BOOKS & LITERATURE 14

QUESTIONS

1. Who wrote 'Tales of the City'?
2. Who wrote over 70 books, including Contraception: its Theory, History and Practice (1923), and Sex and Religion (1929)?
3. When was the first history book, the Great Universal History by Rashid-Eddin of Persia published?
4. In 350 BC Which Greek philosopher wrote 'Meteorologica', the standard textbook on weather for 2,000 years?
5. Who wrote The Great Gatsby?
6. Who wrote 'Green Eggs and Ham'?
7. Who wrote 'Tinker Tailor Solider Spy'?
8. What was the first novel sold through a vending machine – at the Paris Metro?
9. Who was the first English dictionary written by?
10. What is the title of Simone de Beavoir's feminist text?

ANSWERS

1. Armistead Maupin
2. Marie Stopes
3. 1311.
4. Aristotle
5. F. Scott Fitzgerald
6. Dr Suess
7. John le Carre
8. Murder on the Orient Express.
9. Samuel Johnson, in 1755.
10. The Second Sex

ROUND 16
BOOKS & LITERATURE 15

QUESTIONS

1. Who was Poet Laureate from 1984?
2. Which American writer and poet is buried in the churchyard at Heptonstall, West Yorkshire?
3. What is the name of the largest online bookshop?
4. What nationality was Mark Twain?
5. Which Agatha Christie book introduced Hercule Poirot?
6. In 1971 who was created a Dame Commander of the British Empire?
7. Which Agatha Christie stage play holds the record for the longest run ever in London?
8. What is the pen name of American writer and cartoonist Theodor Seuss Geisel best know for his children's book?
9. Who wrote and illustrated 'The Very Hungry Caterpillar'?
10. Who won the Booker Prize in 1982?

ANSWERS

1. Ted Hughes
2. Sylvia Plath
3. Amazon
4. American
5. The Mysterious Affair at Styles, 1920
6. Agatha Christie
7. The Mousetrap
8. Dr. Seuss
9. Eric Carle
10. Thomas Keneally for 'Schindler's Ark'

ROUND 16
BOOKS & LITERATURE 16

QUESTIONS

1. Which Dr. Seuss book was based on a $50 bet he had with a friend that he couldn't write an entire book using only fifty words?
2. What do Hansel and Gretal find a house made of?
3. What are the names of The Brothers Grimm?
4. Which book would you find a Gryphon and a Mock Turtle?
5. Which P G Wodehouse first features Jeeves and Bertie Wooster?
6. Who wrote the poems 'Dulce et Decorum Est' and 'Anthem for Doomed Youth'?
7. In World War I which American novelist won the Silver Medal of Military Valor
8. Which feminist wrote 'Fear of Flying'?
9. Which famous feminist text is written by Germaine Greer?
10. On February 14, 1989, Ayatollah Ruhollah Khomeini, the leader of Iran, issued a fatwa, calling for the death of which novelist?

ANSWERS

1. Green Eggs and Ham
2. Gingerbread
3. Jakob and Wilhelm
4. Alice's Adventures in Wonderland
5. 'The Man with Two Left Feet,' 1917
6. Wilfred Owen
7. Ernest Hemingway
8. Erica Jong
9. 'The Female Eunuch'
10. Salman Rushdie

ROUND 16
BOOKS & LITERATURE 17

QUESTIONS

1. On April 2, 1836 who married Catherine Hogarth, with whom he had ten children?
2. Who won the Booker Prize in 1976?
3. The Pulitzer Prize for Fiction is awarded to writers of what nationality?
4. What year did Harper Lee win a Pulitzer Prize for 'To Kill a Mockingbird'?
5. What book won the Pulitzer Prize for fiction in 1980?
6. What book won the Pulitzer Prize for fiction in 1983?
7. What is this passage from; "One day, about noon, going towards my boat, I was exceedingly surprised with the print of a man's naked foot on the shore…"?
8. What book won the Pulitzer Prize for fiction in 1988?
9. On the 9th June, 1865 which author was involved in the Staplehurst train crash and narrowly escaped death?
10. What book won the Pulitzer Prize for fiction in 1994?

ANSWERS

1. Charles Dickens
2. David Storey for 'Saville'
3. American
4. 1961
5. 'The Executioner's Song' by Norman Mailer
6. 'The Color Purple' by Alice Walker
7. Robinson Crusoe
8. 'Beloved' by Toni Morrison
9. Charles Dickens
10. 'The Shipping News' by E. Annie Proulx

ROUND 16
BOOKS & LITERATURE 18

QUESTIONS

1. What year was Jane Eyre published?
2. Who published his first volume of poems titled Hours of Idleness in 1807?
3. In what year did Trotula, a midwife of Salerno, write 'The Diseases of Women' - which was used in medical schools for 600 years?
4. What year were novels first serialized in English newspapers?
5. In 1819 which historical novel was written by Walter Scott?
6. What is Herman Melville's most famous novel?
7. What year was 'Alice's Adventures in Wonderland' published?
8. Who won the Booker Prize in 1978?
9. British mathematician and author Reverend Charles Lutwidge Dodgson is better know as whom?
10. Which writer has never had any of his novels out of print in England since initial publication?

ANSWERS

1. 1847
2. Byron
3. 1097
4. 1720
5. Ivanhoe
6. Moby Dick
7. 1865
8. Iris Murdoch for 'The Sea, the Sea'
9. Lewis Carroll.
10. Charles Dickens

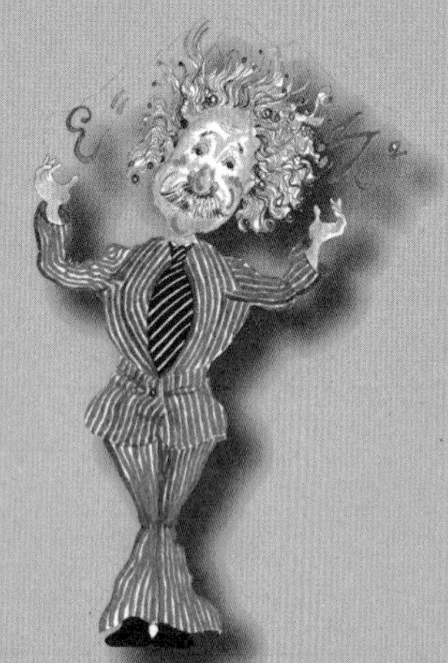

ULTIMATE
BRAINBUSTER

THE BRAINBUSTERS

Two pages of the hardest quiz questions on Earth.

ROUND 17
THE BRAINBUSTERS

QUESTIONS

1. Which eminent palaeontologist was Steven Spielberg's consultant on Jurassic Park?
2. Where did Richard III die?
3. Fernando Hierro joined Real Madrid from which other Spanish team?
4. What massacre is the Dalrymple dynasty associated with?
5. What year was the Beverage Report published?
6. The nearest black hole to Earth in our galaxy is part of which binary system?
7. What is the average daily temperature on Pluto?
8. Michael Jackson was born in which American state?
9. What year was Paypal founded?
10. What is the Spanish name for grouper fish?

ANSWERS

1. Jack Horner
2. Bosworth
3. Valladolid
4. Glencoe
5. 1942
6. Cygnus X-1
7. -220°C
8. Indiana
9. 1998
10. Mero

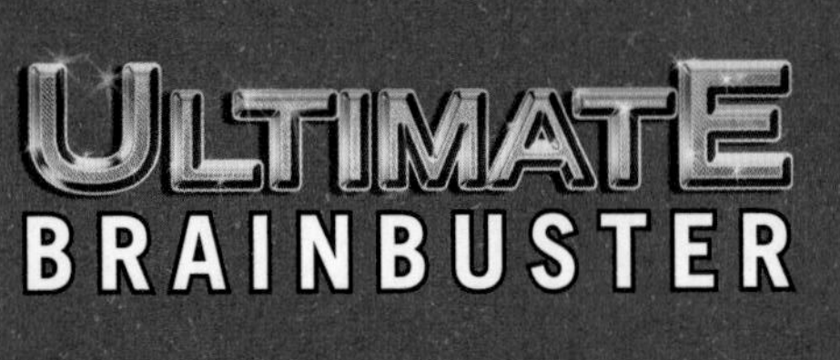

ROUND 17
THE BRAINBUSTERS

QUESTIONS

1. Which motorway links Glasgow and Edinburgh?
2. What year was the first Porsche sports car produced?
3. Who wrote 'All Quiet On The Orient Express'?
4. What was the title of John Lennon's 1974 solo album?
5. The Red Army Faction revolutionaries were known as what?
6. What was the title of the first film Alfred Hitchcock directed?
7. The slogan "A Diamond is Forever", was coined

by which American advertising agency?
8. What is 5625 divided by 15?
9. Which Victorian naturalist came up with the term dinosaurs?
10. Who is the bounty hunter of Star Wars infamy?

ANSWERS

1. M8
2. 1948
3. Magnus Mills
4. Walls and Bridges
5. Bader-Meinhof
6. The Pleasure Garden
7. N.W. Ayer & Son
8. 325
9. Richard Owen
10. Boba Fett